THE WAGE & HOUR HANDBOOK FOR HOTELS, RESTAURANTS, & INSTITUTIONS

The Wage & Hour Handbook for Hotels, Restaurants, & Institutions

ARCH STOKES

CBI

CBI Publishing Company, Inc.
51 Sleeper Street, Boston, Massachusetts 02210

Library of Congress Cataloging in Publication Data

Stokes, Arch Y.
    The wage & hour handbook for hotels, res-
taurants, & institutions.

    Published in 1976 under the title: The wage
& hour law guidebook for hotel, motels, and
restaurants.

    1. Wages–Hotels, taverns, etc.–United States.
2. Wages–Restaurants, lunch rooms, etc.–United
States. 3. Hours of labor–United States.
I. Title.
KF3505.H6S8 1978 344'.73'01284794 78-9278
ISBN 0-8436-2133-8

Printed in the United States of America

*For the hospitable ladies and gentlemen
who own, operate, and manage hotels,
restaurants, and institutions.*

Contents

Preface

Everyone has heard the phrase, "ignorance of the law is no excuse." However, the myriad of new laws and regulations covering every facet of business operations make it increasingly difficult for non-lawyers to avoid violations. Accordingly, CBI is pleased to publish *THE WAGE & HOUR HANDBOOK FOR HOTELS, RESTAURANTS, & INSTITUTIONS,* which covers a major aspect of the Labor Laws regulating the hospitality and foodservice industries.

This newly-revised publication is particularly notable inasmuch as the Federal Wage & Hour Law has been amended to expand its coverage of hotels, motels, and restaurants.

Furthermore, this book is the only complete Wage & Hour Handbook available which includes an appendix summarizing applicable State Wage & Hour Laws.

THE WAGE & HOUR HANDBOOK FOR HOTELS, RESTAURANTS, & INSTITUTIONS is presented from a *preventive law* standpoint based upon legal and practical analyses, extensive trial experience, and numerous seminars and lectures on the subject all over the United States. Most importantly, however, it is written in lay language to enable managers, controllers, and personnel directors to benefit from daily usage.

The publication of this book is indicative of CBI's commitment to *preventive law* to afford our industries the tools to avoid costly lawsuits and administrative complaints which necessarily result from violations.

CBI Publishing Company

Acknowledgments

All Handbooks in the *Stokes Employee Relations Series* published by CBI are products of my firm's commitment to the practice of *preventive law*. Thus, I acknowledge with great appreciation the many progressive hospitality and foodservice companies, public assembly facilities, hospitals and health care centers which allow my firm the privilege of representing them on a *preventive law* basis.

I acknowledge with special appreciation American Hospitality Advisors, Inc., Carlson Companies, Inc., Hilton Hotels Corporation, Holiday Inns, Hyatt Corporation, The Louisiana Superdome, Marriott Corporation, Minnesota Hospitality Association, Omni International Hotels, Inc., Oxford Development of Minnesota, Inc., Radisson Hotel Corporation, San Francisco Hotel Association, The Sheraton Corporation, and Western International Hotels, Inc., for their encouragement, support and assistance.

Foreword

Although volumes of compliance guidelines have been written on the Wage & Hour Laws since the inception of the Fair Labor Standards Act in 1938, nothing as summarily comprehensive and as up-to-date has been evidenced as this Wage & Hour Handbook for our industry by this writer. Arch Stokes, an attorney, presents herein a factual guide to legal compliance within the law in terms that are easily interpreted by non-legal managers.

Extensive experience combined with legal and practical analysis makes this publication particularly notable. It explicitly addresses the pertinent aspects of Wage & Hour Law directly related to hotels, restaurants, and institutions.

The publication of this book is not only indicative of Arch Stokes's knowledge of the law, but evidence of his dedication to an interest in our industry and the dignity of the individuals who are a part of it.

As this publication goes to press, the Wage & Hour Law continues to change, and further detailed amendments are inevitable. Arch Stokes is dedicated to continued follow-up as changes occur.

Richard Smith
Senior Vice President
Hilton Hotels Corporation

1.

OVERVIEW

1-1.   Introduction

Wage & Hour Law is actually a jigsaw puzzle or maze of Federal
and State Laws and regulations. Employers are charged with the
responsibility of implementing those portions of both Federal
and State Wage & Hour Laws which are the most favorable to
employees and the most restrictive on employers.

Example: Several states have eliminated tip credits. In
those states, tip credits may not be taken, even though Federal
Law still permits them. Similarly, Federal Law prohibiting certain forms of child labor takes precedence over State Law, even
though such activity may not be proscribed by State Law.

Thus, this revised and expanded edition not only explains the
basic Federal Wage & Hour Law in lay terms, but also contains a
special appendix summarizing relevant State Wage & Hour Laws.

Additionally, the frequent mobility of managerial and non-
supervisory employees in the hospitality and foodservice industries necessitates a handbook useful in all fifty (50) states and
the District of Columbia.

Therefore, the user should study the basic text and check the
relevant State Wage & Hour Law, if any, to insure complete
compliance.

1

1-2.   Federal Wage & Hour Law

The Fair Labor Standards Act of 1938, as amended [hereinafter referred to as the Wage & Hour Law or the Law], establishes certain minimum wage, overtime, equal pay, record-keeping, and child labor requirements for covered employers.

The Wage & Hour Law is administered by the Wage & Hour Division, Employment Standards Administration, U.S. Department of Labor [hereinafter referred to as the Wage & Hour Division]. Compliance Officers or Specialists (investigators) are authorized to examine an employer's wage policies covered by the Law, either pursuant to an individual complaint or on a "spot-check" basis. Private complainants and the Solicitor of Labor may file Federal lawsuits for recovery of back wages, damages, costs, and attorneys' fees.

The Law applies, regardless of the number of employees or whether they work full- or part-time. It does not, however, require extra pay, premium pay, or days off for Saturdays, Sundays, or holidays. Whether days off or premium rates of any kind are granted depends upon the employment agreement, company policy, collective bargaining agreement, or possibly State Law.

Additionally, employers should realize that the Law does not require vacation, severance pay, or a discharge notice. Moreover, there is no Federal legal limitation on the number of hours of work for individuals sixteen (16) years of age or older, provided the overtime pay provisions are satisfied.

On February 1, 1967, hotels, motels, and restaurants were first subjected to the Wage & Hour Law to a significant degree. However, it was not until the 1974 amendments, effective May 1, 1974 that the hospitality and foodservice industries were covered by such significant provisions as the overtime requirements.

Since the 1974 amendments, the Wage & Hour Division has investigated hotels, motels, and restaurants to a greater extent than in the past. There have been more administrative investigations, rulings and opinions, back wage settlements, lawsuits, and court decisions unfavorable to these industries than in any previous period.

Since both Federal and State Wage & Hour Laws governing the hospitality and foodservice industries are often different from those applying to other industries, it is crucial for employers to understand the basics.

1-3. Age Discrimination & Garnishment

The Wage & Hour Division also enforces the Age Discrimination in Employment Act of 1967, proscribing discrimination and employment practices against individuals between the ages of forty (40) and sixty-five (65). Effective July 1, 1979, the EEOC is the enforcement agency for age discrimination, which, effective January 1, 1979, covers individuals between the ages of forty (40) and seventy (70). Furthermore, Title III of the Consumer Credit Protection Act (Federal Wage Garnishment Law), limiting the amount of an employee's disposable earnings subject to garnishment in any one workweek, is implemented by the Wage & Hour Division.

1-4. Exceptions, Credits, & Exemptions

Whenever an employer may take advantage of an exception, credit, or exemption in discharging his/her responsibilities under Wage & Hour Law, such exception, credit, or exemption is strictly construed, and the burden is always on the employer to prove compliance.

1-5. Amendments to Wage & Hour Laws

There are usually bills pending in the United States Congress and in various states which would, if enacted, *inter alia,* eliminate or reduce tip credits, raise the minimum wage, and require indexing increases and overtime raises. The principles set forth in this Handbook are generally applicable, even if some of the specifics change. However, to avoid misinterpretation, this book will be revised if necessary.

Caveat: This book is a practical summary of selected aspects of Federal and State Wage & Hour Laws as they affect the hospitality and foodservice industries as of January 1, 1979. It is general in nature and application. Accordingly, for specific questions, contact your attorney. Furthermore, it is beyond the scope of this Handbook to cover city, county, or local ordinances on wages and hours.

2.

2-1.   Introduction

The first and foremost question is whether an employer is subject to the Federal Wage & Hour Law. If an employer does not make enough in annual sales to be covered by the Law, then the relevant State Wage & Hour Law may apply. Where the State Wage & Hour Law's provisions are more favorable to employees, State Law generally applies regardless of dollar volume. Accordingly, always check Appendix B for individual State Wage & Hour Laws.

Generally, however, the overwhelming majority of employers can be considered covered by the Law. Once an employer is subject to the Law, a plethora of wage and recordkeeping requirements, restrictions, and liabilities attach to all aspects of an employer's wage policies, practices, and procedures.

2-2.   Hotels and Motels

Q: What are hotels and motels within the meaning of the Law?

A: The term "hotel" means an establishment *primarily engaged in providing public accommodations to transient guests in the form of food, shelter, protection, and entertainment for a reasonable reward.*

Hotels operated by membership organizations open to the public and apartment hotels furnishing public accommodations to transients are all included within this definition.

However, an apartment or residential hotel is not legally considered a hotel unless more than half of its annual dollar volume is derived from providing lodging or lodging and meals to transient guests representative of the general public. Therefore, establishments which do not provide lodging accommodations to the public are not hotels under the Law. Similarly, rooming and boarding houses and private residences operated as tourist homes are also excluded. On the other hand, resort hotels, even if operated seasonally, are hotels for the purposes of coverage and exemptions under the Wage & Hour Law.

An establishment whose income is primarily from providing a permanent place of residence, or from providing residential facilities complete with bedrooms and kitchen for leased periods longer than three (3) months, would not be considered a hotel within the meaning of the Law.

The term "motel" means an establishment which provides services similar to that of a hotel but caters mostly to the motoring public, furnishing automobile parking facilities either adjacent to the room or cabin rented, or at some other easily accessible place. Motor hotels, motor lodges, motor courts, motor inns, tourist courts, tourist lodges, and the like are all included.

2-3.   Restaurants

Q: What is a restaurant under Wage & Hour Law?

A: This question arises since foodservice establishments are treated differently from restaurants under the Law. Restaurants are facilities providing space and service for the consumption of food on the premises, normally at tables, which also afford public patrons an assorted menu.

Example: The Wage & Hour Administrator has commented that hamburger and fried chicken establishments are not restaurants within the meaning of the Wage & Hour Law if they do not provide full service facilities for consumption on the premises, as well as a more varied menu. However, this question is still subject to court interpretation.

Q: Is an establishment still a hotel, motel, or restaurant under the Law even if it derives revenues from other functions?

A: Generally, yes. As long as the primary function of hotels and motels remains public accommodation for travelers in the form of lodging or lodging and meals, their status is preserved.

Example: A hotel which operates a laundry, entertainment lounge, valet shop, gift shop, hobby shop, and the like is still a hotel within the meaning of the Law. Likewise, a hotel which engages in the rental of public rooms for meetings, lectures, banquets, dances, trade exhibits, weddings, etc., will also be considered a hotel for Wage & Hour Law purposes.

2-4. $275,00 in Gross Sales

Q: Which establishments are covered by Wage & Hour Law?

A: Any hotel, motel, restaurant, or private institutional employer who grosses $275,00 in annual sales as of July 1, 1978. The following chart illustrates the jurisdictional increases from 1977 to 1982:

Effective Date	*Annual Gross Dollar Volume*
January 1, 1977	$250,000
July 1, 1978	$275,000
July 1, 1980	$325,000
January 1, 1982	$362,500

Since the dollar volume increases will eliminate certain smaller employers from coverage, Congress specified that those employers who cease to be covered because of the increase cannot reduce an employee's wage rate below the minimum wage in effect before the increase. Furthermore, such employer cannot stop his/her adherence to the Wage & Hour Law's overtime provisions for previously covered employees. On the other hand, the employer does not have to pay the minimum wage or overtime pay to employees hired after the effective date of the increase.

Example: An employer with annual sales of $270,00 as of January 1, 1978, cannot, upon the effective date (July 1, 1978) of the increase in the dollar test to $275,000, reduce an employee's wage rate below the minimum in effect prior to July 1, 1978. An employee hired after July 1, 1978, may be compensated at a rate less than the Federal minimum wage, provided, however, the employer does not have annual gross sales of $275,000, and the applicable State minimum wage is satisfied.

2-5.   Golf Course

Q: Is a resort hotel's golf course covered by the same provisions of the Law as the other hotel facilites?

A: Generally, yes. If the hotel or motel has its own golf course adjacent to the facility and operates it as part of the hotel or motel establishment, then the same provisions apply. Therefore, the golf course employees would be treated the same as the other hotel employees for the purposes of the Wage & Hour Law.

Note: The compliance responsibility of a golf course operator with respect to caddies, where the golf course activities are included in *enterprise* coverage of the hotel or motel, is unsettled. The Wage & Hour Division is of the opinion that the golf course operator would be required to pay caddies in accordance with the Law's provisions only if they are the operator's employees under the Wage & Hour Law. The Wage & Hour Division is not prepared to rule that a golf course caddy is necessarily an employee within the meaning of the Law.

Golf courses operated at different locations from the hotel are generally considered separate establishments. Therefore, if open to the general public, the golf course may qualify for an exemption from the monetary provisions for seasonally operated amusement or recreational establishments.

3.

WORKWEEK & HOURS WORKED

3-1.   Introduction

The determination of an employee's "hours worked" within a particular standard "workweek" is the most basic matter relevant to whether an employer is in compliance with the Wage & Hour Law. If an employer does not master this concept through the implementation of its wage policies, practices, and procedures, the Wage & Hour Division Compliance Officer will discover this fact at the outset of the investigation.

Each workweek stands alone. Accordingly, each employee's hours worked are computed on an individual workweek basis. Similarly, the employee's regular hourly rate of pay is determined on an individual workweek basis depending on the hours worked and method of compensation for that week.

Recordkeeping depends upon an employer's ability accurately to compensate employees for all hours worked within a given workweek. Otherwise, any records which an employer may present for justification of its policies may be inaccurate and useless.

Therefore, it is fundamental to Wage & Hour Law to recognize what portions of an employee's time constitute hours worked within that particular employee's given workweek.

9

3-2.   Workweek

Q: What is a "workweek"?

A: The term "workweek" means a regularly recurring period of 168 hours during seven (7) consecutive twenty-four-hour (24) periods.

The workweek need not coincide with the calendar week. It may begin any day of the week and at any hour of the day.

Each workweek stands alone, and employment for two or more workweeks cannot be averaged for the sake of computing overtime or minimum wages. The minimum wage must be paid for every hour worked in each workweek, and overtime must be paid for all hours worked in excess of the maximum workweek applicable to the type of employment in which the employee is engaged.

Generally, coverage and application under the Law are determined on a workweek basis.

3-3.   Salaried Employees

Q: How is the hourly rate computed for weekly salaried employees?

A: It will, of course, depend on the employment arrangement. If the employee works a regular workweek, the number of hours divided into the salary equals the regular hourly rate.

On the other hand, if the employment agreement clearly states that for a fixed salary an employee works whatever hours are necessary and the workweek fluctuates, then the salary divided by the actual hours worked equals the regular rate of pay for that particular workweek. The employer is still obligated to pay one and one-half times the regular rate of pay for all hours worked over forty-six (46) hours, as of May 1, 1975 [over forty-four (44) hours for maids and custodials after May 1, 1976 and over forty (40) hours for maids and custodials after May 1, 1977]. As of January 1, 1978, overtime must be paid after forty-four (44) hours, and after forty (40) hours as of January 1, 1979. See Chapter 5 for a detailed discussion of overtime pay requirements.

Q: How is the hourly rate computed for monthly salaried employees?

A: If a salary is for one-half a month, it is multiplied by twenty-four (24) and the product divided by fifty-two (52) to get the weekly equivalent. Similarly, a monthly salary is multiplied by twelve (12) and divided by fifty-two (52).

3-4.   Two Separate Jobs

Q: How is the hourly rate computed for employees who work two separate jobs? For example, a housekeeper who works as a banquet waiter during the same workweek.

A: If the work is performed for the same employer, the second job is paid at time and one-half for time worked beyond forty (40) hours.

3-5.   Donated Time

Q: Does an employer have to pay a worker who voluntarily continues to work at the end of a shift or one that reports early and works voluntarily?

A: Yes. Work not requested, but suffered or permitted is considered work time or hours worked.

Example: Waiters or waitresses who finish service but stay beyond their regular shift may create an overtime situation. The employer should either shorten the workweek or make sure they get off the premises when their normal work time is over.

Q: How can an employer be held responsible for employees working outside their designated hours and against the orders and rules of the employer?

A: The Wage & Hour Division takes the position that in all cases it is the duty of management to exercise its control to insure that work is not performed which the employer does not want performed. An employer cannot accept the benefits for such donated work time without compensating employees accordingly. The mere promulgation of a rule against such work is not enough. Management has the power to enforce work schedules, shifts, and rules, and must make every effort to do so.

3-6.   Waiting Time

Q: Are employers required to pay employees for waiting time?

A: Waiting time is compensable if the employee must remain on hand until work has been prepared for the employee. On the other hand, the employee who is waiting to be hired or waiting voluntarily to see if work will be available need not be compensated for such waiting time.

3-7.   Mealtime

Q: Is time spent during meal periods considered work time?

A: Generally, mealtime is not compensable if employees are allowed a complete, uninterrupted thirty (30) minutes to eat. On the other hand, mealtime is counted as time worked if employees must work during the meal period.

Example: Assistant chefs, sous chefs, cooks, waiters, waitresses, bus help, and the like who are not given a full thirty (30) minutes to eat must be paid for that time. The employer cannot lawfully deduct thirty (30) minutes per day for mealtime unless the employee is in fact free from duties and not subject to call.

3-8.   Changing and Washing Time

Q: **Must an employer compensate employees for changing and washing time?**

A: Generally, yes. An employee who must change into or out of an employer's uniform on the hotel, motel, or restaurant premises before or after working must be paid for such time. If it is necessary for the performance of the employee's job, the employee must be compensated for the time spent changing clothes and washing for work.

The employee's changing and washing time is not compensable if it is expressly excluded from time worked by a *bona fide* collective bargaining agreement, or by the custom or practice under it. Likewise, if the employee changes or washes only for the employee's convenience, it need not be counted as time worked.

3-9.   Travel Time

Q: **Does the Law require that employees be paid for travel time?**

A: Employees must get paid for travel time if they drive a vehicle or ride as a helper in the employer's business or if they have to travel from job to job, site to site during a regular workday. In some instances, time spent carrying heavy or bulky packages to or from the post office also counts as time worked. Employees on trips away from home overnight, traveling during regular working hours, must be compensated for that time.

Travel time is not compensable for travel to the job in the morning and from the job at the end of the day. Also, an employee who travels as a passenger outside the employee's working hours need not be compensated.

4.

4-1.   Introduction

All employers should be aware that they are required to insure that employees are paid at least the minimum wage for all hours worked in a given workweek. Again, check your State's Wage & Hour Law as the State Minimum Wage may be higher than the Federal Law.

Employers are also charged with knowledge of the applicable minimum wage.

4-2.   Rates

Q: What is the applicable minimum wage?

A: The following schedule of minimum wage increases covers the period from 1976 to 1981:

January 1, 1976	$2.20
January 1, 1977	$2.30
January 1, 1978	$2.65
January 1, 1979	$2.90
January 1, 1980	$3.10
January 1, 1981	$3.35

Q: What does the Law require concerning the payment of the minimum wage?

A: The Wage & Hour Law does not require that an employee be paid each week. The employer may make wage or salary payments at other regular intervals, such as every two weeks, every half month or once a month. What the Law does require is that both minimum wage and overtime pay must be computed on the basis of *actual hours worked* with each workweek standing alone.

Q: Are meals, lodging, and other facilities customarily provided to employees considered part of the employer's payment of wages?

A: Generally, yes. The reasonable cost or fair value of these items would normally be added to the employee's regular hourly wage rate for the purpose of computing overtime pay. Such benefits can be excluded from the term "wage" pursuant to the provisions of a *bona fide* collective bargaining agreement.

Note: See Chapters 5, 6, & 7 on credits that an employer may take in meeting the minimum wage provisions of the Law.

4-3.   Central Office Employees

Q: Does an employer have to pay a higher minimum wage to any employee?

A: No. As of January 1, 1978, the minimum wage is the same for central office employees as for other hotel and food-service employees. If an employee works for more than a single hotel, motel, or restaurant within the enterprise, such employee is considered a central office employee.

Example: An employee who does accounting work for two establishments of the chain X of Motels in City Y is a central office employee.

5.

OVERTIME

5-1.   Introduction

Employers are required to pay overtime at the rate of time and one-half an employee's regular hourly rate for all hours worked in excess of the applicable workweek. A single workweek is the standard, and therefore, the Law does not permit averaging of hours over two or more weeks. This is the case regardless of whether an employee works on a standard or irregular shift schedule and regardless of whether pay is on a daily, weekly, bi-weekly, monthly, or other basis.

Generally, employees cannot waive or give up their rights to overtime pay, regardless of the documentation.

Overtime pay violations are the most common cause of employee complaints to the Wage & Hour Division. Therefore, it is extremely important to know when to pay overtime and at what rate.

Note: An employee's standard hourly rate as set by the employer or pursuant to a *bona fide* collective bargaining agreement is not necessarily that employee's *regular rate of pay* for overtime pay computation purposes. His/her *regular hourly rate of pay* may be increased by various benefits given by the employer and considered to be remuneration under the Wage & Hour Law.

Example: Free meals provided at the employer's expense may raise an employee's rate of pay according to the value of meal per hour.

16

Hence, to avoid inadvertently building up back overtime pay liability, check this matter carefully.

5-2.   May 1, 1974 and January 1, 1978

Q: When is overtime pay required?

A: The hospitality and foodservice industries were not legally obligated to pay overtime (other than pursuant to a State Law, company policy, or contract) until May 1, 1974. On this date, every hotel, motel, and restaurant employee covered by the overtime pay provisions of the Wage & Hour Law had to be paid overtime.

Of course, many companies have always had to pay central office employees overtime for all hours worked in excess of forty (40) per workweek. Similarly, numerous hotels, motels, and restaurants have paid overtime pursuant to company policy or a collective bargaining agreement.

However, until May 1, 1974, most hotel, motel, and restaurant employees have been exempt from Federal overtime pay requirements. These industries are gradually losing this special treatment.

As of January 1, 1978, most employees within the hospitality and foodservice industries must be paid overtime at the rate of time and one-half their regular hourly rates of pay for all hours worked in excess of forty-four (44) per workweek, and effective May 1, 1977, maids and custodial employees have been paid overtime for all hours worked over forty (40) per week.

Effective January 1, 1979, all employees must be paid overtime after forty (40) hours worked within the standard workweek.

Q: When does an employer have to pay earned overtime pay to employees?

A: There is no Federal requirement that overtime compensation be paid weekly. Generally, overtime pay earned in a given workweek must be paid on the regular payday for the period in which the workweek ends.

However, if the correct amount of overtime pay cannot be determined until some time after the regular pay period, the employer must pay the overtime compensation as soon thereafter as practicable. *Payment may not be delayed longer than is necessary for the employer to compute and arrange for payment.* Moreover, in no case may payment be postponed beyond the next day after such computation is made.

5-3.   Schedule

Q: What is the overtime schedule?

A: The following chart illustrates the overtime schedule, *i.e.,* time and one-half for all hours worked in excess of:

May 1, 1975	46 (all employees)
May 1, 1976	44 (only maids and custodials)
May 1, 1977	40 (only maids and custodials)
January 1, 1978	44 (other than maids and custodials)
January 1, 1979	40 (all employees)

Thus, beginning May 1, 1976, all maids and custodial employees were treated more favorably than other hospitality and food-service employees; moreover, as of May 1, 1977, this group was treated like employees in other covered industries with respect to overtime. As of January 1, 1979, there is no distinction as to overtime and minimum wages between the hospitality and other industries.

5-4.   Time and One-Half the Regular Rate of Pay

Q: Does overtime pay always mean time and one-half the minimum wage?

A: Not necessarily. The Law requires overtime at NOT LESS THAN TIME AND ONE-HALF THE EMPLOYEE'S REGULAR RATE OF PAY (which must be at least the minimum wage).

Example: Thus, if an employee is paid at a straight-time rate of $3.00 per hour, then the overtime rate is $4.50 per hour for each hour of overtime.

Q: What is an employee's regular rate of pay for overtime computation purposes?

A: The regular rate includes all remuneration for employment except for certain payments and benefits specifically excluded by the Law.

Example: Payments which usually are not part of the regular rate of pay for overtime computation purposes are:

(1) Reimbursement for expenses incurred on the employer's behalf;
(2) Premium payments for "daily overtime" or for work on Saturdays, Sundays, and holidays;
(3) Gifts and payments in the nature of gifts on special occasions;
(4) Payments for occasional periods when no work is performed due to vacation, holiday, illness, or disability;
(5) Discretionary bonuses;
(6) Pay for certain idle hours;
(7) Report-in, show-up or call-back pay;
(8) On-call pay where the employee is not called;
(9) Payments made by an employer to a *bona fide* profit-sharing and thrift or saving plans; and
(10) Payments made to a *bona fide* plan for providing old-age retirement, life, accident, or health insurance, or similar benefits, such as SUB.

Thus, the regular rate of pay for overtime computation purposes is determined by dividing an employee's *total remuneration* for employment (except for the exclusions) in any workweek by the total number of hours actually worked in the workweek.

Example: Where payments are made to employees in the form of goods or facilities, *e.g.,* meals and lodging, which are regarded as part of wages, the reasonable cost or fair market value of such goods or facilities must be included in the employee's regular rate of pay for the purposes of computing overtime. Furthermore, nondiscretionary, guaranteed, or automatic bonuses must be included in earnings to determine the regular rate.

Note: There are bills pending in Congress which would increase the overtime rate from time and one-half to two and one-half times an employee's regular rate of pay.

5-5.   Collective Bargaining Agreements and Regular Rate of Pay

Q: What effect, if any, does a collective bargaining agreement have on the determination of an employee's regular rate of pay for overtime computation purposes?

A: Such an agreement has a very significant and often decisive effect. The Law specifically allows management and the union to agree to exclude certain benefits from an employee's regular rate of pay, if particularly excluded in the collective bargaining agreement. Therefore, it is very important to analyze relevant collective bargaining agreements to insure that there is a provision, section, paragraph, clause, or article specifically defining an employee's regular rate of pay. This definition should definitely exclude all forms of remuneration, *other than the established wage rate*, from an employee's regular rate of pay.

Caveat: If a collective bargaining agreement does not limit the regular rate of pay to the established wage rate, the contract may become evidence of a Wage & Hour Law violation.

Example: A collective bargaining agreement should include language similar to the following:

Article 7, REGULAR RATE OF PAY, HOURS OF WORK, OVERTIME & PREMIUM PAY

§22. *Regular Rate of Pay.* It is specifically agreed by the UNION and HYATT that any meals, uniforms, rooms, and/or laundering and maintenance of uniforms and other remuneration provided or furnished by HYATT to an employee shall not be considered as part of the employee's regular rate of pay for overtime computation purposes within the meaning of Wage & Hour Law; and that an employee's regular rate of pay is that rate respectively reflected on the Schedule of Wages in the Appendix covering that employee's job classification, subject to Sections 20 and 30 covering probationary rates.

5-6.   Custodial Employees

Q: What are custodial employees?

A: Generally, custodial employees include the following:

Watch Personnel	Maintenance Employees
Guards	Night Cleaners
Housekeepers	Linen Deliverers
Janitors/Janitresses	Laundry Employees
Porters	Gardeners and Yard Employees
Housekeeping Aides	Room/House Attendants

5-7.   Overtime for Salaried Employees

Q: What is the general rule on overtime for salaried employees?

A: If an employee is employed only on a weekly salaried basis, the regular hourly rate of pay on which time and one-half must be paid is computed by dividing the salary by the number of hours for which the salary is intended to compensate.

A semi-monthly salary is computed into an hourly rate by first arriving at the equivalent weekly wage by multiplying times twenty-four (24) and dividing by fifty-two (52).

See the rules for exemptions from overtime in Chapter 8.

Q: How should nonexempt salaried employees who work more than forty hours a week be compensated if their hours fluctuate from workweek to workweek?

A: An employee working a fluctuating workweek may be paid a salary pursuant to an agreement with the employer that the employee will receive a fixed amount as straight-time pay for whatever hours may be worked in a workweek, regardless of whether the employee works few or many.

Where there is a *clear agreement* between the parties that the fixed salary is compensation (apart from overtime pay) for all hours worked each workweek, whatever their number, such a salary arrangement is lawful if the amount of the salary is sufficient to provide the minimum wage rate for each hour worked in those workweeks in which the number of hours an employee works is the greatest. *Additionally, the employee must receive overtime compensation for all hours worked in excess of the applicable standard workweek at a rate of not less than one-half the regular rate of pay.*

The regular rate of the employee will vary from workweek to workweek and is determined by dividing the number of hours worked in the workweek into the amount of the salary to obtain the applicable hourly rate for the particular workweek. Payment for overtime hours at one-half such rate in addition to the salary satisfies the overtime pay requirement because such hours have already been compensated at the straight time rate under the salary agreement.

Note: The *fluctuating workweek* method of overtime pay may not be used unless the salary is sufficiently large to insure that no workweek will be worked in which the employee's average hourly earnings from the salary fall below the minimum wage applicable under the Wage & Hour Law *and* unless the employee clearly understands and agrees that the salary covers whatever hours the job may demand in a given workweek. Also, the employer must pay the salary even though the workweek was one in which a full schedule of hours is not worked.

This method results in different amounts of compensation depending upon the hours worked in excess of the standard workweek.

Example: If Hotel Z employs Hourly Cook X who works a fluctuating workweek, the Hotel decides to enter into an agreement with X to pay X a fixed salary for all hours worked regardless of the number. The agreement also provides that the salary does not cover overtime compensation, which will be paid at the rate of one-half the straight-time rate for each workweek in addition to the salary. Hotel Z's standard workweek is forty (40) hours, Z is bound by its decision to pay overtime after forty (40) hours.

Hourly Cook X is paid a weekly salary of $140.00 to compensate X for all hours worked but not including overtime compensation at the rate of one-half X's straight-time rate for each week. X works the following hours during the course of four consecutive weeks and should be compensated accordingly:

1. 46 = $200 + $13.04 [$2.17(1/2 × $4.35) × 6hrs. O/T] = $213.04
2. 56 = $200 + $28.64 [$1.79(1/2 × $3.57) × 16hrs. O/T] = $228.64

3. 50 = $200 + $20.00 [$2.00(1/2 X $4.00) X 10hrs. O/T] = $220.00
4. 60 = $200 + $33.40 [$1.67(1/2 X $3.33) X 20hrs. O/T] = $233.40

Note: Hourly Cook X never works more than sixty (60) hours per workweek. Also recognize that X's hourly rate of pay for the purpose of computing overtime fluctuates depending upon the number of hours worked.

Q: Is it permissible to pay a fixed salary for varying workweeks including overtime pay?

A: Generally, no. However, there is an exception to this rule. Section 7(f) of the Law is the only provision allowing an employer to pay the same total compensation each workweek to an employee who works overtime and whose hours vary from week to week.

Section 7(f) provides that no employer shall be deemed to have violated the overtime pay provisions of the Law by employing an employee for a workweek in excess of the applicable maximum-hours standard if the following requirements are met:
(1) The employee is employed pursuant to a *bona fide* individual contract or pursuant to an agreement made as a result of collective bargaining by representatives of employees;
(2) The duties of such employees necessitate irregular hours of work; and
(3) The contract or agreement (a) specifies a regular rate of pay which is not less than the applicable statutory minimum wage, (b) provides for compensation at a rate of not less than one and one-half times the specified rate for all hours worked in excess of the maximum hours standard in any workweek, and (c) provides a weekly guarantee of pay covering compensation based on the specified regular and overtime rates for not more than sixty (60) hours.

Caveat: This type of contract should be drafted only after a careful legal and factual analysis of the actual duties and hours of the employees sought to be covered by such an arrangement. Every method of overtime compensation for salaried, nonexempt employees should be established very clearly to the employee so both parties understand both the literal and practical effects.

6.

TIP CREDIT

6-1.   Introduction

Tipping is obviously an integral part of the hospitality and food-service businesses. Employers and employees alike anticipate tips as an important part of employee income.

The Senate Committee on Labor and Public Welfare in its report of the bill on the 1974 amendments to the Wage and Hour Law, stated:

> The Committee re-examined the role of tips as wages and the concept of allowing tips to be counted as part of the minimum wage. The Committee reviewed the study of tips presented to the Congress by the Department of Labor in 1971 as well as provisions of State minimum wage laws which permit the counting of tips toward a minimum wage.
>
> The Committee was impressed by the extent to which customer tips contributed to the earnings of some hotel and restaurant employees in March 1970 (the date of the Labor Department survey). After reviewing the estimates in this report, the Committee was persuaded that the tip allowance could not be reduced at this time, but that the tipped employee should have stronger protection to ensure the fair operation of this provision.

The Industry Wage Survey of the Bureau of Labor Statistics of the U.S. Department of Labor reported on the effect of tips on the earnings of employees in hotels, motels, and restaurants as of June, 1973 for twenty-four metropolitan areas.

The report concluded that tips contributed substantially to the earnings of employees in a number of hotel and motel service occupations, particularly those paid comparatively low wages by employers such as customer lodging attendants or bell personnel, waiters, and waitresses, and their foodservice assistants (busboys and busgirls).

The survey showed that employer-paid wages for table waiters and waitresses in full-course restaurants averaged lower than wages paid their foodservice assistants in twenty-three of the twenty-four areas studied. On the other hand, when customer tips were added to wages paid, total hourly earnings averaged *more* for waiters and waitresses than for their assistants. Bartenders usually averaged the highest in total hourly earnings, but rarely received forty percent (40%) or more of their earnings in tips. Waiters and waitresses in cocktail lounges followed next in average hourly earnings, but received substantially larger proportions from customer tips.

This survey clearly supports the position taken by the Congress in connection with the 1974 amendments when it provided for a tip credit of up to fifty percent (50%).

The U.S. Department of Labor 1971 report on tips included the following highlights:

Eating and Drinking Places
1. Tip earnings constitute the most important source of hourly income for the majority of tipped workers in covered eating and drinking places. When tips are added to the cash wage of tipped employees, the average hourly cash wages paid by the employer accounted for only 42 percent of the combined $2.89 average hourly earnings. Thus, customer generosity is a critical component in earnings of tipped employees.
2. The survey data clearly show that the utilization of that provision of the FLSA which permits an allowance of up to 50 percent of the minimum wage for tips actually received in arriving at the cash wage of a tipped employee, and the deduction of the reasonable cost of employer furnished perquisities, had a marked effect on the hourly cash wages of tipped employees as well as on the average hourly wage bill cost to employers of these workers;

Three-fourths of the tipped employees in the survey and four-fifths of all waiters and waitresses were paid cash wages of less than $1.45 an hour. Maximum use of the tip allowance was made for 17 percent of tipped employees. In all regions of the country, except the West, more than half of the tipped employees were paid cash wages at least 25 cents below the $1.45 minimum wage applicable to covered nontipped employees.

Elimination of the tip allowance would have required a 22 percent increase in the March 1970 hourly wage bill of the 323,900 employees in the three selected occupations in establishments with tipped employees to raise the cash wages for the 281,800 employees who were paid less than $1.45 an hour to that level. In the South the increase would have been 45 percent. Even in the relatively high wage Northeastern region, elimination of the tip allowance would have meant a 22 percent increase in the hourly wage bill.

Year-Round Hotels and Motels

1. Like covered eating and drinking places, tipped employees in covered year-round hotels and motels received substantial proportions of their total hourly compensation in tips rather than wages. When estimated tips were added to the cash wages of tipped employees, average hourly cash wages paid by the employer accounted for less than half of their combined $2.72 average hourly earnings.

2. Although seven-tenths of the tipped employees had combined average hourly cash wages and tips of $2.00 or more an hour, only one-sixth of the nontipped employees in the same occupations in tipping establishments earned as much as $2.00 an hour. Two-fifths of the nontipped workers were at the minimum wage applicable to their employment.

3. The inclusion of chambermaids as a tippable occupation in hotels and motels had the effect of raising average cash wages and lowering the estimated average hourly tips of tipped employees because employers were required to pay most of them at least $1.45 an hour since they did not qualify for the tipping allowance. In tipping establishments, only one-eighth of the chambermaids qualified as tipped employees—received more than $20.00 a month in tips—and in establishments with no tipped employees, chambermaids comprised nine-tenths of the labor force in the five selected occupations.

4. The tip allowance and employer furnished perquisites had a marked effect on the hourly cash wages of tipped employees and on the average hourly wage bill cost to employers of these workers;

Two-thirds of all tipped employees were paid less than $1.45 an hour, as were four-fifths of the tipped waiters and waitresses. Because of the 50 percent tip allowance, 14 percent of the tipped employees were paid approximately half of the statutory $1.45 an hour minimum wage in March 1970. In all regions except the West, 40 percent or more of the tipped employees were paid cash wages at least 25 cents below the $1.45 minimum wage applicable to nontipped workers.

Elimination of the tip allowance and raising the wages of all employees earning less than $1.45 an hour to that level would have required an 11 percent increase in the hourly wage bill of the 164,400 employees in the selected occupations in covered hotel and motel establishments. Wage increases would have had to be given to 60,300 employees. The wage bill increase was substantially higher in the South (18 percent) but about the same in the Northeast and North Central regions.

5. As in eating and drinking places, there was a negative correlation between average hourly cash wages and estimated average hourly tips of tipped employees. Tipped employees paid cash wages of less than $.75 an hour received estimated average hourly tips of $1.57 an hour, and those paid cash wages of between $1.25 and $1.45 an hour received estimated average hourly tips of $1.16 an hour.

6. The estimated hourly wage bill increase required to raise the cash wages of tipped employees in the five selected occupations in covered year-round hotels and motels paid less than $.80 an hour—the net minimum wage assuming maximum use of the 50 percent tip allowance—and nontipped employees paid less than $1.60 an hour to those levels was three percent for the United States as a whole and five percent in the South. The new minimum will require wage raises for 31 percent of the tipped and nontipped employees in the selected occupations. Based on the March 1970 wage structure, the estimated cost of raising the wages of nontipped employees from $1.45 to $1.60 an hour and eliminating the tip allowance, thereby raising the minimum nonfarm employees subject to the Fair Labor Standards Act, would require an increase of 17 percent and would affect 66 percent of the employees in the five selected occupations.

These reports reflect the impact of tipping within the hospitality and foodservice industries, as well as the importance of the tip credit.

Therefore, the Federal Law currently recognizes the practice of tipping and allows employers to take a tip credit in order to help discharge their legal responsibility to meet the minimum wage.

Caveat: Several State Wage & Hour Laws prohibit tip credits and quite a few limit tip credits to an amount less than that permitted by Federal Law.

Since the tip credit is an exception to the general rule that an employer must pay the full minimum wage, the legality of any tip credit scheme is always strictly construed.

Moreover, it is essential that employers understand the prerequisites for taking a lawful tip credit since there must be strict compliance before a tip credit will be allowed. Please be advised that if an employer is not lawfully taking a tip credit, the entire scheme will be invalidated and back wage liability will necessarily include all amounts of money which had previously been considered tips.

Example: Recently, several foodservice operations were ordered to pay thousands of dollars in back pay (unpaid minimum wages) to waiters/waitresses who had received no pay other than their tips. This arrangement was held illegal, even though the waiters/waitresses received more tips than the amount of the current minimum wage.

6-2.   Tip

Q: **What is a tip within the meaning of the Wage & Hour Law?**

A: A tip is a voluntary gratuity left by a customer for the performance of the individual who is the tipped employee. *Whether to tip and in what amount must be determined at the customer's discretion.*

Q: **What is the tip credit?**

A: It is a method by which an employer is allowed to credit up to fifty percent (50%) of the applicable minimum wage with reported or earned tips in order to discharge the employer's responsibility to pay the minimum wage. The tip credit schedule is as follows:

Effective	Min. Wage	Max. Tip Credit	Cash Wage
Jan. 1, 1978	$2.65	50% or $1.32	$1.33
Jan. 1, 1979	$2.90	45% or $1.30	$1.60
Jan. 1, 1980	$3.10	40% or $1.24	$1.86
Jan. 1, 1981	$3.35	40% or $1.34	$2.01

Q: **Is the tip credit an automatic setoff against the cash wage due an employee?**

A: No. An employer is permitted to take up to the applicable percentage, not an automatic maximum. The employer has the burden of proving to the Wage & Hour Division that the tipped employees actually make the amount of tip credit taken.

6-3.   Requirements for Lawful Tip Credit

Q: What are the requirements for taking a lawful tip credit?

A: An employer may not lawfully take a tip credit unless:

(1) It is in fact a tip and not a service charge;
(2) The employer has informed each tipped employee of the tip credit provision;
(3) All tips received by tipped employees are retained by them (either individually or through a lawful tip pooling arrangement); and
(4) The employee is a tipped employee under the Law.

Q: What is the test to determine who is a tipped employee?

A: An employee engaged in an occupation wherein he or she customarily and regularly receives more than $30.00 per month in tips is a tipped employee within the meaning of the Wage & Hour Law.

6-4.   Tip Records & Reports

Q: How can employers support tip credits?

A: The tip credit must be based on employee reports, tipping practices, and receipts in the establishment. RECORDS AND REPORTS are essential to document and support any position under the Law.

The Wage & Hour Division will require that the employer prove any tip credit taken with adequate tip records.

IRS FORM 4070 (Employee's Report on Tips) must be utilized by employees tipped at least $30.00 per month or more. Employees must also be notified that their employer is taking a tip credit. The following suggested notice may help stimulate more complete tip reporting by employees:

Employees Must Report Tips

Federal Law requires each service employee to report to their employer all tips amounting to $30.00 a month or more. It also requires the employer to add the amount reported in each case to the employee's earned wage and then deduct the Federal social security tax from the employee's total earnings, including tips.

Effective January 1, 1979, the minimum wage is $2.90 per hour. Federal Law authorizes the employer to take up to forty-five percent (45%) of the minimum wage or a maximum of $1.30 per hour as a tip credit toward the minimum wage, if tips received are retained by the tipped employee.

Report all earned tips accurately.

Note: Both the American Hotel & Motel Association and National Restaurant Association have posters in this regard, although neither contains notice provisions on Equal Pay or Child Labor, as does the Federal Wage & Hour poster. See Appendix A.

Accordingly, the Federal and any applicable State posters should be prominently displayed.

The following suggested form may be stamped or printed on the back of each timecard (or time sheet) and signed and executed by each tipped employee at the end of every pay period:

I hereby attest that for the workweek(s) in this pay period I have earned on an hourly basis tips which average an amount equal to the maximum amount of tip credit allowed to be deducted by State or Federal Law. Additionally, I have earned $_____ in tips which I request that you report as additional wages for Federal Income Tax purposes.

_____

Signature of Employee and Date

More elaborate forms should be used for daily records of tips.

Q: Whose responsibility is it to compute tips—the employer's or employee's?

A: Under the Law, it is the employee's responsibility to report all tips earned. Likewise, under Federal Tax Law, the employee is required to report all tips earned. However, as a practical matter the employer is charged with the responsibility of supporting any tip credit taken. An employer must be able to prove in fact that an employee earns in tips at least the amount necessary for the tip credit. Employers can of course take a tip credit up to fifty percent (50%) of the minimum wage if the employee makes that amount, regardless of whether the employee is accurately reporting tips.

Caveat: The Internal Revenue Service promulgated more stringent tip recordkeeping requirements with respect to credit card tips. Controllers and Accounting Directors should study these rules carefully.

Q: What are common methods for recording tips?

A: The following four methods are frequently used:

(1) Credit card tips;
(2) A percentage of a patron's or guest's cash expenditure;
(3) The number of carries by employees in bell service or the number of covers by waiters or waitresses; and
(4) Employee's certification of tips earned on the back of the timecard or on the tip sheet.

6-5.   Overtime for Tipped Employees

Q: How does an employer determine the overtime rate for tipped employees?

A: *The overtime rate is always time and one-half the regular rate of pay.* The regular rate of pay of tipped employees includes the amount of tip credit taken, but not the excess amount of reported tips. Remember that the regular rate also includes the reasonable cost or fair value of meals and lodging, unless specifically excluded pursuant to the provisions of a *bona fide* collective bargaining agreement.

Example: Where an employer takes a forty-five percent (45%) tip credit and pays $1.30 per hour in cash wages, that employee must receive a cash wage of $3.05 per hour for each hour of overtime pay, but not greater than *forty-five percent (45%) of the minimum wage* as of January 1, 1979, and forty percent (40%) as of January 1, 1980. Employers are not permitted to a tip credit of forty-five percent (45%) of the overtime rate.

6-6.   Tip Pooling

Q: What is the rule on tip pooling arrangements?

A: The Wage & Hour Division has issued the following interpretative instruction to its Compliance Officers on tip pooling:

Field Operations Handbook

30d04 Tip Pooling. (a) The requirement that an employee retain all tips does not preclude voluntary arrangements for tip splitting or pooling among employees who customarily and regularly receive tips, *e.g.,* waiters, bellhops, waitresses, countermen, busboys, service bartenders, etc. A valid tip pooling arrangement would include only employees who participate directly in rendering in the service area, the service for which the tips are given, and not such employees as janitors, dishwashers, chefs, and laundry room attendants. *It is not required that the particular busboys and others who share in tips must receive tips from customers.*

(b) Employees who share in tips are tipped employees if they receive at least $30 a month in tips. In such case, the tip credit may be taken. Payment of more than 50 percent (50%) of the minimum wage as necessary is required when the tips and the maximum tip credit fail to meet the full minimum wage.

(c) *Tip credit may not be taken if the tip pooling system is a mandatory requirement of the employer and not voluntary with the employee.* If the employer coerces the employees into adopting a pooling system against their will, the tipped employees are not being permitted to retain all their tips. Thus, one of the 3(m) requirements is not met.

(d) A new employee's acceptance of employment is an establishment with an ongoing, valid tip pool arrangement will, as a general rule, be considered to be the result of voluntary agreement on his/her part.

(e) Any plan for pooling or splitting tips which has been adopted since the effective date of the 1974 amendments (5/1/74) should be closely scrutinized. It has been found that a number of plans have been designed to circumvent the Act's requirements. For example, some plans require that tipped employees turn over a percentage of their tips (sometimes involun-

tarily) to the employer and such tips are used to pay the wages of other employees who were not previously in a tip pool and who do not usually receive tips. In such and similar cases, the facts should be submitted through channels to the Assistant Administrator for the office of Fair Labor Standards for resolution.
(Italics supplied.)

Caveat: There are bills pending in the U.S. Congress and in various State Legislatures which would reduce or eliminate tip credits.

POST ACCEPTABLE NOTICES INFORMING EMPLOYEES OF THE TIP CREDIT, MINIMUM WAGE, AND OVERTIME REQUIREMENTS

The Wage & Hour Division has published a bulletin on tipped employees which is reproduced in Appendix A, along with other Federal publications.

7.

COMPENSATION OF BANQUET PERSONNEL

7-1.   Introduction

Generally, tip credits are unlawful for many reasons if taken in the usual "banquet gratuity" situation; the most important being that banquet gratuities in the hospitality and foodservice industries are generally service charges within the meaning of the Wage & Hour Law and not tips.

7-2.   Banquet "Gratuity" Is a Service Charge

Q: Can an employer take a tip credit for what is customarily known in the industry as a "banquet gratuity"?

A: The general rule adhered to by the Wage & Hour Division is that service charges are not tips. Therefore, according to the Wage & Hour Division, a set percentage service charge (sometimes called a "gratuity") established in advance by the management is not a tip within the meaning of the tip credit definition. Again, whether to tip and, if so, in what amount is to be determined by the customer.

Q: Why is this so significant to the hospitality and foodservice industries?

A: Since the general rule as interpreted by the Wage & Hour Division makes it unlawful for an employer to take a tip credit for banquet service charges, two things result:

(1) Employers must pay banquet personnel at least the minimum wage without taking a tip credit; and
(2) The hourly rate of pay of the banquet waiter, for example, includes the minimum wage paid by the employer plus whatever his percentage of the service charge is.

Therefore, if this individual works overtime, the employer is bound to pay overtime at the rate of one and one-half times his hourly rate for that week; this may be $6, $7, $8 or more per hour, unless the *employer utilizes the "commissioned" employee exemption.*

Q: Are there other reasons the Wage & Hour Division would interpret a banquet service charge as not authorizing a tip credit?

A: Yes. Normally, the entire percentage of the banquet service charge does not go to the regularly tipped nonsupervisory banquet employees. Therefore, it does not satisfy one of the basic conditions for taking a tip credit.

Example: Many establishments charge a fifteen-percent (15%) service charge or "gratuity", and, moreover, a portion of this fifteen percent (15%) is distributed to the "tipped" banquet employees and a portion is retained by management. This necessarily disqualifies such a system for a tip credit.

Q: Is it possible under any circumstances for an employer to take a tip credit in compensating banquet employees?

A: Yes. However, for the purpose of this Handbook, suffice it to say that it is a complex problem, and any lack of compliance with the technical requirements of the Wage & Hour Law may result in costly litigation.

Q: Why is this interpretation of the Law such a shock to those in the hospitality and foodservice industries who have been customarily taking credits from banquet employees for years?

A: Initially, the problem is not as evident until one reaches the question of overtime, *i.e.,* what is a banquet employee's regular hourly rate of pay for a given week for the purpose of computing overtime? Since the hospitality and food-service industries were not required by law to pay overtime until May 1, 1974, many still do not appreciate the impact of the 1974 amendments to hotels, motels, and restaurants.

Secondly, banquet personnel traditionally make very good incomes and are not as likely to complain to the Wage & Hour Division about their pay as other job classifications.

7-3.   A Safe Solution

Q: What is a safe solution?

A: A safe approach to avoid violating the Wage & Hour Law as interpreted by the Wage & Hour Division is the following:

(1) Pay banquet employees at least the minimum wage plus whatever portion of the service charge to which management will agree; and
(2) Eliminate overtime for banquet employees either through scheduling or by treating them as "commissioned" employees exempt from overtime.

7-4.   "Commissioned" Employees Exempt from Overtime

Q: Is it lawful to treat banquet employees as exempt from overtime as other "commissioned" employees?

A: Yes, if all of the following tests for this exemption as provided in Section 7(i) of the Law are satisfied. Section 7(i) paraphrased states that no employer shall be deemed to have violated the overtime pay requirements by employing any employee of a retail or service establishment for a workweek in excess of the applicable workweek specified therein, if:

(1) The regular rate of pay of such employee is in excess of one and one-

half times the minimum hourly rate applicable to such employee; and
(2) More than half the employee's compensation for a representative period (not less than one month) represents commissions on services.

In determining the proper method of compensation representing commissions, all earnings resulting from the application of a *bona fide* commission rate shall be deemed commissions on goods or services without regard to whether the computer commissions exceed the draw or guarantee.

Please note that some State laws do not recognize the commissioned employee exemption.

8.

MISCELLANEOUS CREDITS—MEALS, LODGING AND UNIFORMS

8-1.   Introduction

An employer can take other credits towards the minimum wage so long as no profit is made on the items credited.

The most frequent items for which employers take credits are meals, lodgings, and uniform maintenance. Again, it is necessary to maintain accurate documentation to support these credits.

8-2.   Meals and Lodging

Q: **Can an employer take credit for meals and lodging furnished an employee?**

A: Yes. The recent developments of the Wage & Hour Law do not change the rules with regard to meals and lodging. The employer may take a credit for the *reasonable* cost of meals and lodging furnished an employee. One must base the determination on good accounting practices and not make a profit.

There is no need for an analysis of the employer's "reasonable cost" of meals and lodging if the meal and lodging credit does not reduce the employee's hourly rate of pay below the minimum wage for a given week.

Q: **Are costs of meals and lodging included as part of the employee's wages for overtime pay purposes?**

A: Yes, except to the extent such costs are excluded from wages pursuant to the terms of a *bona fide* collective bargaining agreement.

8-3.   Uniform Maintenance

Q: Can an employer require employees to purchase and maintain uniforms?

A: Yes, but the cost to an employee of furnishing (or paying a security deposit) and laundering uniforms, where required by the employer or the nature of the employment, may not reduce the employee's wages below the minimum wage.

Example: Where an employee works forty (40) hours per week at $3.00 an hour and earns $120.00 (as opposed to $116.00 per week under the applicable 1979 minimum wage of $2.90 an hour), $4.00 could be deducted from the employee's pay before the minimum wage is reduced. Therefore, the problems relating to the cost of furnishing and laundering uniforms affect only those employees who are paid at or near the statutory minimum wage.

Q: What is the "rule of thumb" regarding the cleaning of uniforms?

A: Absent special circumstances, the Wage & Hour Division will consider that it costs approximately one hour's wages per week for an employee to clean and maintain a uniform.

Q: What special circumstance would affect the "one-hour-a-week" rule?

A: As one example, if a collective bargaining agreement contains a provision on this point, then the amount in the agreement would be used. As another illustration, if the employer uses a laundering or rental service, then the actual cost of the service would be used.

Where the employees clearly spend more than an hour a week in uniform maintenance *or* where the employer can clearly establish that less than an hour a week is spent, the actual cost will be used.

Q: What is a uniform?

A: The Wage & Hour Division has ruled that if the pre-scribed clothing is ordinary, basic street clothing (variations are permitted), then it is not a "uniform"; the purchase and main-tenance is solely attributable to the employee. However, a tuxedo is not considered basic street clothing. Similarly, skirts and blouses which must meet the employer's specifications of color, style, and quality would not be basic street clothing.

9.

EXEMPTIONS

9-1. Introduction

Employers do not have to keep certain hourly time records for certain employees and pay minimum wages or overtime pay to those employees considered exempt. The Wage & Hour Law exempts a few categories of employees relevant to hotels, motels, and restaurants. These are the so-called "white collar" exemptions.

Employers should recognize that all exemptions are very strictly construed, and one must clearly satisfy the requirements to be exempt. Job titles and descriptions are never conclusive as to the exempt status of an employee, since Wage & Hour Compliance Officers examine in detail actual job duties and performance.

Example: Management trainees are generally not exempt. *The rule is well established that those training for exempt positions are not exempt during training, unless they are actually performing exempt duties* (such as during an advanced stage of the training program).

The following discussion covers the general rules for exempt employees, however, a particular employee's exemption must be scrutinized on a case-by-case basis.

41

9-2.   Executive Exemption

Q: What criteria must an employee satisfy to be executively exempt from the minimum wage and overtime pay provisions of the Wage & Hour Law?

A: The activities and salaries of those employees must meet certain standards. If they do, such employees are exempt from both the minimum wage and overtime requirements of the Law. This exemption is very strictly interpreted and applied.

EXECUTIVES	*Primary duty:* Manages an enterprise or department subdivision thereof.
General Criteria:	*Supervision:* Customarily and regularly directs work of two or more other employees.
	Salary: $155 or more a week.
	Authority: Can hire and fire or suggest changes in status of other employees.
	Discretion: Customarily and regularly exercises discretionary powers.
	Nonexempt Work: Nonexempt work performed by an executive in a retail or service establishment must be less than forty percent (40%) of his/her weekly hours; nonexempt work performed by any other executive may not exceed twenty percent (20%) of his weekly hours.
	Execptions: There is no limitation as to employees who are in charge of an independent establishment or physically separated branch, or who own a twenty percent (20%) interest in business.
Shorter Test for $250-a-Week Employees:	*Duties:* Same as above
	Supervision: Same as above
	Salary: $250 or more a week, exclusive of board, lodging or other facili-

ties; in Puerto Rico and Virgin Islands, $200 per week.

These executives may perform work not directly related to their exempt executive duties, not to exceed fifty percent (50%) of their working time.

If their salary is $250.00 a week or over (exclusive of board and lodging), they may perform such work up to forty-nine percent (49%) of their working time.

Regardless of salary, fifty percent (50%) of their working time must be spent in executive duties in order to keep their exemption.

Examples of an Executive's Exempt Duties:

(1) Interviewing, selecting, and training employees;
(2) Setting and adjusting pay rates and work hours;
(3) Directing work;
(4) Keeping production records of subordinates for use in supervision;
(5) Evaluating employees' efficiency and productivity;
(6) Handling employees' complaints;
(7) Disciplining employees;
(8) Planning work;
(9) Determining techniques;
(10) Distributing work;
(11) Deciding on types of merchandise, materials, supplies, machinery, or tools;
(12) Controlling flow and distribution of merchandise, materials, and supplies;
(13) Providing for safety of employees and property.

Examples of Nonexempt Duties:

(1) Performing the same kind of work as employees under his supervision;
(2) Performing any production work, even though not like that performed by employees under him, which is not part of his supervisory functions;
(3) Making sales, replenishing stocks, returning stock to shelves, except for supervisory training or demonstration purposes;

(4) Performing routine clerical duties, such as bookkeeping, billing, filing, and operating business machines;

(5) Checking and inspecting goods as a production operation, rather than as a supervisory function;

(6) Keeping records for employees not under his supervision;

(7) Preparing payrolls;

(8) Performing maintenance work;

(9) Repairing machines, as distinguished from an occasional adjustment;

(10) Cleaning around machinery, rearranging displays, and taking an employee's place at the workbench, or on the sales floor.

9-3.   Administrative Exemption

Q: What criteria are necessary to take advantage of the administrative exemption?

A: An employee may qualify as an administrative employee exempt from the minimum wage, overtime, and record-keeping provisions of the Wage & Hour Law, provided certain salary and other standards are fulfilled.

ADMINISTRATIVE EMPLOYEES

Primary Duty: Performs office or nonmanual work relating to management policies, or general business operations of employer or employer's customers.

General Criteria:

Other Duties: Regularly and directly assists a proprietor, an executive, or an administrative employee, *or*

Works under only general supervision along specialized or technical lines, requiring special training, experience or knowledge, *or*

Executes under only general supervision special assignments and task.

Discretion: Customarily and regularly exercises discretion and independent judgment.

Nonexempt Work: Nonexempt work performed by an administrative employee in a retail or service establishment must be less than forty percent (40%) of his weekly hours; nonexempt work performed by any other administrative employee is limited to twenty percent (20%) of his weekly hours.

Salary or Fee: $155 or more a week, exclusive of board, lodging, or other facilities; in Puerto Rico, Virgin Islands, $130 per week.

Shorter Test for $250-a-Week Employees:

Primary Duty: Same as above.

Discretion: Exercises discretion and independent judgment and performs office work directly related to management responsibility or the general operation of employer's business.

Salary or Fee: $250 or more a week, exclusive of board, lodging, or other facilities; in Puerto Rico and Virgin Islands, $200 per week.

Examples of Types of Administratively Exempt Employees:

(1) Executive and administrative assistants, such as executive secretaries, assistants to the general manager, confidential assistants, and the like.

These employees assist an executive or general manager in responsible duties but do not themselves necessarily have executive authority.

(2) Staff employees who are advisory specialists for management, such as tax, insurance, and sales research experts; wage rate analysts; investment consultants; and heads of one-person departments, such as credit managers, purchasing agents, buyers, safety directors, personnel directors, and labor relations directors.

(3) Those who perform special assignments, often away from their employer's place of business, such as management consultants, lease buyers, etc.

Some relevant classifications which must be examined against these criteria to determine exempt or nonexempt status are:

Assistant Housekeeper	Chief Security Officer
Assistant Maître d'	Night Manager
Chef and Assistant or	Assistant Auditor
Sous Chef	General Cashier
Chief or Assistant Chief Engineer	Paymaster
Steward and Assistant Steward	Head Front Office Cashier
Head Bartender	Front Office Manager
Banquet Set-Up Supervisor	Head Checker
Head Door Service	Chief Telephone Operator
Superintendent of Services	Sales Department Personnel
Credit Manager	Catering Director
Entertainment Director	

Many of the above classifications often perform the duties of those they supervise, *e.g.,* assistant housekeepers, inspectresses, assistant maître d's, captains, etc., and the forty percent (40%) and forty-nine percent (49%) limitations could be endangered.

Sales department personnel are on working time if they return to the hotel to entertain clients at dinner. If they travel on hotel business during normal working hours, travel time is work time.

It is recommended that one document working hours for out-of-town business trips, *i.e.,* calling on travel agents, or servicing a trade show, and produce a memo in the file at the time of return. Attendance at local travel agent receptions and similar evening cocktail parties can generally be considered working time.

9-4.   Professional Exemption

Q: What are the requirements to be exempt as a so-called professional employee?

A: An employee may qualify for the professional exemption provided the following salary and other standards are fulfilled:

PROFESSIONAL
EMPLOYEES

Primary Duty: Performs work requiring scientific or specialized study, as distinguished from apprentice training and training for routine work, *or*

Performs original and creative work in a recognized artistic endeavor, depending primarily on the invention, imagination, or talent of the employee, *or*

Teaches, tutors, instructs, or lectures in the activity of imparting knowledge, and is employed and engaged in this activity as a teacher certified or recognized as such in the school system or educational establishment by which he is employed.

General
Criteria:

Other Duties: Performs work predominantly intellectual and varied (not routine) which cannot be standardized in point of time.

Discretion: Consistently exercises discretion and judgment.

Nonexempt Work: Limited to twenty percent (20%) of professional employee's weekly hours worked.

Salary or Fee: $170 or more a week, exclusive of board, lodging

	or other facilities; in Puerto Rico and Virgin Islands, $150 per week.

Shorter Test for
$250-a-Week
Employees:

Primary Duty: Same as above.

Discretion: Consistent exercise of discretion and judgment required with respect to scientific, specialized, or academic work, but not with respect to artistic endeavors.

Salary or Fee: $250 or more a week, exclusive of board, lodging or other facilities; in Puerto Rico and Virgin Islands, $200 per week.

Examples of Professionally Exempt Employees: Attorneys, physicians, nurses, accountants, actuaries, engineers, architects, teachers, chemists, biologists, pharmacists, medical technologists, etc. The areas in which the professional exemption may be available are expanding. As knowledge is developed, academic training is broadened, degrees are offered in new, diverse, and pragmatic fields, and specialties are created.

The true specialist who is given new and greater responsibility comes closer to meeting the professional exemption. Thus, various legal and medical technical specialists (paralegals and paramedics) may develop the high degree of skill, responsibility, and judgment necessary to satisfy this exemption. Moreover, systems analysts in the data processing field may be exempt as professionals.

9-5.   Outside Sales Employee Exemption

Q: **Will salespeople in the hospitality and foodservice industries qualify for the outside sales exemption?**

A: The Wage & Hour Division has not issued any general rule on this question, although several Area Directors of the Wage & Hour Division have specifically ruled that lower level sales "managers" are not exempt, primarily because they do not regularly work away from the employer's premises.

Q: What are the requirements for this exemption?

A: An outside sales employee is one who makes sales away from the employer's place of business. Inside sales work is not exempt.

The following requirements must be fulfilled in order for the sales employee to be exempt:

(1) *One is employed for the purpose of, and customarily and regularly works away from the employer's place of business;*
(2) Obtaining orders or contracts for services or use of facilities such as radio time, advertising, and typewriter repairs. Selling these services when performed away from the employer's establishment is exempt; performing them is not exempt work; and
(3) The employee's hours of work in activities other than those described above do not exceed twenty percent (20%) of the hours worked in the workweek by nonexempt employees of the employer.

There is no salary limitation for the outside sales exemption. Also, one should note that when these requirements were promulgated, it appears that the Wage & Hour Division did not consider the salespeople in the hospitality and foodservice industries who are engaged in sales on the employer's premises. At any rate, a strict interpretation and application of these exemptions would probably exclude hotel, motel and restaurant salespeople therefrom.

Q: Is there any other way to exempt salespeople from overtime?

A: Yes. It is possible to treat them as "commissioned" employees within the meaning of Section 7(i) of the Law. See discussion at end of Chapter 6 above.

AUDIT EXEMPT EMPLOYEES' ACTUAL DUTIES
SALARY REQUIREMENTS WILL BE PERIODICALLY RAISED

10.

CHILD LABOR

10-1.   Introduction

The Child Labor provisions of the Wage & Hour Law are being enforced rigorously, especially since the 1974 amendments authorize severe civil penalties that may be assessed administratively.

Child Labor prohibitions are complicated and comprehensive, covering ages, occupations, and hours of work of children. Employers who regularly employ individuals eighteen (18) years of age or younger must be cognizant of these rules.

Q: What is the general rule on Child Labor?

A: The Child Labor provisions of the Wage & Hour Law give Federal protection to children from possible harmful effects of industrialization by prohibiting "oppressive Child Labor" where interstate activities and covered enterprises are concerned. The prohibition applies to all of the activities of a "covered enterprise" under the Wage & Hour Law.

10-2.   Minimum Ages and Occupations

Q: What are the minimum ages required by the Law?

A: In general, the Law requires a minimum age of sixteen (16) years. However, certain non-agricultural occupations declared hazardous by the Wage & Hour Division are foreclosed to children under eighteen (18) years of age. Currently, there are seventeen occupations listed as hazardous for persons sixteen (16) to eighteen (18) years old. Those occupations particularly relevant to hotels, motels, and restaurants are:

(1) The operation of power-driven bakery machinery;
(2) Certain types of motor vehicle driving,
(3) The operation and maintenance of power driven machines, band saws, and guillotine shears;
(4) Roofing operations; and
(5) The operation of elevators and other power-driven hoisting apparatus, except that it is not prohibited for sixteen-(16) or seventeen-year-old-(17) minors to operate an automatic elevator.

Q: May persons between the ages of fourteen (14) and sixteen (16) be employed under any circumstances?

A: Persons between the ages of fourteen (14) and sixteen (16) may be employed in foodservice and gasoline service establishments in the following positions:

(1) Office and clerical work, including the operation of office machines;
(2) Cashiering, selling, modeling, art work, work in advertising departments, window trimming, and comparative shopping;
(3) Price marking and tagging by hand or by machine, assembling orders, packing, and shelving;
(4) Bagging and carrying out customers' orders;
(5) Errand and delivery work by foot, bicycle, and public transportation;
(6) Clean-up work, including use of vacuum cleaners and floor waxers, and maintenance of grounds, but not including the use of power-driven mowers or cutters;
(7) Kitchen work and other work involved in preparing and serving food and beverages, including the operation of machines and devices used in the performance of such work, such as, but not limited to, dishwashers, toasters, dumb waiters, popcorn poppers, milkshake blenders, and coffee grinders;
(8) Work in connection with cars and trucks if confined to the following— dispensing gasoline and oil, courtesy service, car cleaning, washing, and polishing, and other positions permitted in this list, but not including work involving the use of pits, racks, or lifting apparatus, or involving

the inflation of any tire mounted on a rim equipped with a removal retaining ring; and

(9) Cleaning vegetables and fruits, and wrapping, sealing, labeling, weighing, pricing, and stocking goods when performed in areas physically separate from those where the following work is performed: work in freezers and meat coolers, and all work in connection with the preparation of meats for sale.

Q: Are there hourly restrictions on the employment of persons between fourteen (14) and sixteen (16) years of age?

A: Yes. Minors fourteen (14) and fifteen (15) years old may not be employed:

(1) During school hours;
(2) Before 7:00 a.m. or after 7:00 p.m. from June 1 through Labor Day;
(3) More than three (3) hours a day on school days;
(4) More than eighteen (18) hours a week during school weeks;
(5) More than eight (8) hours a day on non-school days; and
(6) More than forty (40) hours a week in non-school weeks.

Q: What occupations in the retail, foodservice or gasoline service establishments are specifically prohibited by the Federal regulations?

A: Persons between the ages of fourteen (14) and sixteen (16) *may not* be employed in retail, foodservice, or gasoline service establishments in any of the following occupations:

(1) Work performed in or about boiler or engine rooms;
(2) Work in connection with maintenance or repair of the establishment, machines, or equipment;
(3) Outside window washing that includes working from window sills, and all work requiring the use of ladders, scaffolds, or their substitute;
(4) Cooking (except at soda fountains, lunch counters, snack bars, or cafeteria serving counters) and baking;
(5) Occupations which involve operating, setting up, adjusting, cleaning, oiling, or repairing power-driven food slicers and grinders, food choppers and cutters, and bakery-type mixers;
(6) Work in freezers and meat coolers, and all work in the preparation of the meats for sales (except wrapping, sealing, labeling, weighing, pricing, and stocking when performed in other areas);

(7) Loading and unloading goods to and from trucks, railroad cars, or conveyors; and

(8) All occupations in warehouses except office and clerical work.

Q: What does an employer do if State and Federal Child Labor Laws are in conflict?

A: The general rule is that an employer must comply with the more restrictive law.

10-3.   Penalties

Q: What are the penalties for violations of the Federal Child Labor Law?

A: Under the 1974 amendments to the Wage & Hour Law any person who violates the provisions relating to Child Labor, or any of the regulations promulgated under the Law, will be subject to a *civil* penalty or not more than $1,000.00 *for each violation.* In assessing the amount of the penalty, the size of the company and the gravity of the violation will be taken into consideration.

This is a new penalty and should not be confused with the criminal penalty that has previously existed and is still authorized for violations of Child Labor Laws. The criminal penalties provide for a fine of $10,000.00 for the first offense and a fine of $10,000.00 and six months in jail for the second offense. *Furthermore, the new civil penalty can be imposed by the Secretary of Labor without resorting to court action.*

Q: What is an illustration of noncompliance under the new Law that could make an employer subject to the new $1,000.00 civil penalty?

A: Where State "A" has a Child Labor Law stating that during school you can work fourteen-(14) and fifteen-year-old (15) children twenty (20) hours each school week, and the Federal Law limits such hours to eighteen (18) hours per week, an employer is subject to the civil penalty of $1,000.00 if he works his fourteen-(14) and fifteen-year-old (15) employees twenty (20) hours a week.

10-4.   Age Certificates

Q: What can an employer do to protect himself against possible violations?

A: Age certificates are a defense against unintentional violations of the Wage & Hour Law, but only if they certify as to Federal standards. However, State certificates are acceptable in a large majority of cases. State employment or age certificates are accepted under the Wage & Hour Law as proof of age in forty-five states, the District of Columbia, and Puerto Rico. Federal certificates of age are obtainable in four other states, *i.e.,* Idaho, Mississippi, South Carolina, and Texas. In Alaska and Guam, birth certificates, and baptismal and census records have the status of Federal certificates of age.

Employers will be fully protected against unintentional violations of the Federal Child Labor provisions and regulations if they have on file *unexpired age certificates issued pursuant to the regulations.*

An age certificate is an official statement of a child's age based on the best available documentary evidence of age and signed by the child and the issuing officer. If there is a possibility that a job applicant is under age for the contemplated work, an age certificate should be obtained. The 1974 amendments to the Wage & Hour Law require employers to obtain proof of age from employees.

A State age certificate is a defense to a Federal Child Labor Law violation *only* if it shows the child to be above the minimum age fixed by this law for the occupation for which he is employed. If a lower age is permitted by State Law, a certificate showing that the child is of the age required for state purposes is no protection to the employer under the Wage & Hour Law.

Q: Are there any exemptions from the Child Labor provisions of the Wage & Hour Law?

A: The Wage & Hour Law exempts the following three categories from its Child Labor, minimum wage, equal pay, and overtime pay provisions:

(1) Children who deliver newspapers to consumers;
(2) Homeworkers engaged in making evergreen wreaths, including harvesting of the evergreens; and
(3) Individuals employed in foreign countries or in overseas areas that are exempted from the geographical scope of the Wage & Hour Law.

These are the only Child Labor exemptions that are expressly combined with wage exemptions. The first two exemptions are lost in any workweek in which a child devotes part of his working time to other work which is within the scope of the Wage & Hour Law and not exempt from the Child Labor restrictions.

Q: Are there any exemptions which apply to the Child Labor provisions of the Wage & Hour Law?

A: The following categories are exemptions only from the Child Labor provisions, and do not relieve an employer of the duty to comply with the minimum wage, equal pay, overtime pay, and recordkeeping requirements:

(1) Non-farm fourteen-(14) and fifteen-year-old (15) employees;
(2) Parental non-farm employment—the general rule that no child under sixteen (16) years may be employed in any non-agricultural occupation does not apply where a parent, or a person standing in place of a parent, employs his own child, or a child in his custody, in any occupation the Secretary of Labor has found to be hazardous;
(3) Theatrical employment—children of any age may be employed as actors or performers in motion pictures or theatrical productions, or in radio or television productions; and
(4) Agricultural employment outside of school hours.

PENALTIES FOR CHILD LABOR LAW VIOLATIONS ARE SEVERE.

11.

STUDENTS

It is usually permissible under both Federal and State Wage & Hour Laws to pay full-time students less than the current minimum wage once subminimum wage rate certificates or authorizations are obtained from the applicable administrative agency. The Secretary of Labor issues such certificates to allow the employment of full-time students at eighty-five percent (85%) of the minimum wage, so long as working time does not exceed twenty (20) hours in a workweek.

There is no Federal subminimum wage rate generally applicable to youth.

An employer may hire up to six (6) students without prior certification; provided, the employer certifies that the hiring of students will not displace other workers.

If an employer desires to employ more than six (6) full-time students at the lower rate, he/she must first follow the certification procedures set out in the Law and applicable regulations.

Q: May students be employed at a lower rate than the normal minimum wage?

A: Yes, under certain conditions, *full-time* students may be employed at eighty-five percent (85) of the applicable minimum wage. They must be *full-time,* not part-time, students based upon the classification given by the institution. These students may be employed no more than twenty (20) hours a week, EXCEPT DURING VACATION PERIODS.

One may employ up to six (6) full-time students working part-time during school sessions and full-time during vacation periods by applying to the nearest office of the Wage & Hour Division of the U.S. Department of Labor and certifying that their employment will not interfere with full-time employment opportunities. To employ seven (7) or more, one needs "full-time student certificates" from the nearest regional office of the Department of Labor. Generally, however, the Department of Labor has been allowing employers to employ as many full-time students at eighty-five percent (85%) of the minimum wage as equals ten percent (10%) of the total employee hours calculated monthly.

Q: Are there any age limitations on who is a full-time student?

A: No. Anyone, any age, who qualified as a full-time student according to the classification of the institution may be paid eighty-five percent (85%) of the minimum wage.

Q: During vacation periods, can an employer work a full-time student full-time and pay only eighty-five percent (85%) of the minimum wage?

A: To some extent, yes. However, this eighty-five percent (85%) rule only applies up to forty (40) hours a week. Thus, the following method of computation is applicable to a certified full-time student working fifty (50) hours a week during a vacation period:

First 40 hours - 85% minimum wage
     6 hours - 100% minimum wage
     4 hours - 150% minimum wage

12.

EQUAL PAY

12-1. Introduction

Equal pay for equal work is a concept of Wage & Hour Law enacted in 1963 to guarantee that pay differentials for substantially similar jobs would not be based on the sex of the employee.

Many collective bargaining agreements contain equal pay violations in the language and/or wage schedule. These obvious violations should be corrected as soon as practicable.

Equal pay violations can be particularly expensive, since this form of sex discrimination will also result in a violation of Title VII of the Civil Rights Act of 1964, as amended. Therefore, employees can complain to both the Wage & Hour Division and the U.S. Equal Employment Opportunity Commission about equal pay violations. As of 1979 the EEOC enforces the Equal Pay Act.

12-2. Equal Pay for Equal Work Rule

Q: What is "equal pay for equal work" rule?

A: *No employer shall discriminate between employees on the basis of sex* by paying wages to employees at a rate less than that paid to employees of the opposite sex for equal work on jobs which require equal skill, effort, and responsibility, and which are performed under similar working conditions. The rule is contained in the Equal Pay Act of 1963, which was an amendment added to the Wage & Hour Law.

Q: What are limitations of the "equal pay for equal work" rule?

A: The jobs must require the performance of equal skill, effort, and responsibility and be under similar working conditions. Furthermore, the pay differential between male and female employees is not violative of the equal pay provisions of the Wage & Hour Law if the differential is based upon a seniority system, a merit system, a system which measures earnings by quantity or quality or production, or any other factor other than sex.

12-3.   Equal Pay Problem Areas

Q: What jobs in hotels, motels, and restaurants have resulted in equal pay problems?

A: For examples, see the following list:

Room and House Attendants
Maids and Housemen
Bartenders and Barmaids
Waiters and Waitresses
Male and Female Sales Managers
Busboys and Busgirls
Male and Female Foodservice Unit Managers

Q: What should employers do?

A: First, eliminate all pay differentials between males and females performing substantially equal work by raising the lower paid employees of one sex to the rate of the other sex.

Second, all job classifications should be changed to a neuter form.

Third, supervisors must be apprised of the serious consequences for violations of this rule. The Department of Labor has already recovered millions of dollars in equal pay violations.

Fourth, post any applicable equal pay policy or poster for all to see and encourage them to read it.

Q: Is a violation of the equal pay portions of the Wage & Hour Law considered sex discrimination?

A: Yes. Therefore, such a violation could be investigated both by the U.S. Equal Employment Opportunity Commission (EEOC) or the applicable State agencies, and by the Wage & Hour Division, if a complaint is filed with both agencies. This makes an equal pay violation tremendously expensive.*

POST EQUAL PAY POLICY

*See The Equal Opportunity Handbook for Hotels, Restaurants & Institutions.

13.

AGE DISCRIMINATION

13-1. Introduction

The Age Discrimination in Employment Act of 1967 proscribes all forms of discrimination in employment practices against individuals between forty (40) and seventy (70) years of age.

Employers should appreciate that this law is separate from the Wage & Hour Law, although it too is administered by the Wage & Hour Division. As of 1979, the EEOC administers the Age Discrimination Act.

Q: What constitutes age discrimination?

A: Any employment practice which results in discriminatory treatment of persons between the ages of forty (40) and seventy (70) constitutes age discrimination. It is unlawful to fail or refuse to hire, discharge, reduce wages, or otherwise discriminate because of age against those between forty (40) and seventy (70).

13-2. Coverage

Q: Are all employers covered by the Age Discrimination in Employment Act, if they are covered by the Wage & Hour Law?

A: Not necessarily. Employers have to employ twenty or more persons to be subject to the Age Discrimination in Employment Act of 1967. Although not an amendment to the Fair Labor Standards Act, the age discrimination law is administered by the EEOC as of 1979.

13-3. Examples

Q: **What are some examples of age discrimination?**

A: A few common examples are:

(1) Using terms such as "boy", "girl", "young", or the like in advertisements.
(2) Firing or refusing to hire employees such as desk clerks, cocktail waitresses, etc., between the ages of forty (40) and seventy (70) in order to create or preserve a "youthful image."

Q: **Can an employer allow younger workers to work more overtime hours than older workers?**

A: No. Such an allocation of overtime is illegal unless a statutory exception applies.

Q: **Can an employer refuse to hire a person because he is not receiving Social Security payments?**

A: No. It is illegal for an employer to specify that he will hire only persons receiving Social Security benefits.

Q: **Can a worker be retired before age seventy (70) against his wishes?**

A: Generally not, except if such involuntary retirement is required by the terms of a *bona fide* retirement or pension plan, and that requirement is tied into the funding of the plan.

Q: **Are validated employment tests permissible for job applicants?**

A: Yes. However, such a test must be specifically job related, as well as fair, reasonable, and administered in good faith without age discrimination. Furthermore, proper validation is often difficult to prove.

Q: Is it permissible to give preference to a job applicant who is forty-one (41) years old over a sixty-one (61) year old applicant solely on age?

A: No. It is just as unlawful to give preference to one person over another *within* the forty (40) to seventy (70) protected age group as it is to give preference because of age to someone under forty (40) over someone between forty (40) and seventy (70).

Q: What should an employer do to avoid age discrimination violations?

A: Although it is almost impossible to prevent all such charges, it is recommended that employers do the following:

(1) Educate supervisors;
(2) Post the age discrimination poster in a prominent place and require that it be read; and
(3) Conduct audits periodically to check for violations.

13-4.   Basis for Age Discrimination Law

Q: Upon what statistical information does the Wage & Hour Division base its enforcement of the age discrimination provisions?

A: Initially, the employer's statistical information on those individuals between forty (40) and seventy (70) who *were not* hired or promoted, or who *were* hired, terminated, or promoted, etc., is considered by the Wage & Hour Division.

Additionally, the Wage & Hour Division promotes the following results of employment studies:

(1) Older workers' attendance is likely to be better than that of younger employees;
(2) Older workers are less prone to change jobs;

(3) The output of older persons up to age seventy (70) compares favorably with that of younger workers in production jobs;

(4) There are minimal differences in output in professional jobs;

(5) Learning ability does not decline significantly with age;

(6) Although some older workers may have longer periods of illness, they are apt to be ill or disabled less frequently than younger persons;

(7) Older workers are highly motivated as evidenced by their job stability and their attitude of job responsibility.

13-5.   Executive Exemptions

Q: Are executives exempt from the Law's increased upper age limit from sixty-five (65) to seventy (70)?

A: Yes, if the following conditions are met:

(1) The executive is a top-level employee who for the two years prior to retirement is in a *bona fide* high policymaking or executive position;

(2) The executive is entitled to an immediate arrival nonforfeitable retirement benefit which is the equivalent of a straight-life annuity of $27,000.

AGE BIAS CLAIMANTS ARE ENTITLED TO JURY TRIALS
POST AN AGE DISCRIMINATION POSTER

14.

RECORDKEEPING

14-1.   Introduction

Once an employer implements wage policies consistent with the basics of Wage & Hour Law, the next question concerns whether the employer can *prove* the wage policies are within the law.

Obviously, the most important ingredients for proving compliance are *records which accurately reflect the facts, i.e., correct pay for actual hours worked.*

The Wage & Hour Law requires that certain facts be recorded, but it does not dictate what form must be used. Therefore, employers are free to establish and maintain their own recordkeeping systems. This should be done not only in accordance with accounting needs, but also pursuant to a policy of *Preventive Law.*

Q: What records are required to be kept by employers?

A: The recordkeeping requirements are complicated. Although no particular form of records is required, *some* of the specific recordkeeping items that must be maintained are:

(1) Name of employee in full;
(2) Home address, including zip code;
(3) Date of birth, if under nineteen (19);
(4) Sex and occupation;
(5) Time of day and day of week on which the employee's workweek begins;
(6) Regular hourly rate of pay in any workweek in which overtime pre-

mium is due, and basis of wage payment (such ad $3 hr., $20 day, $110 wk., $100 wk. plus five percent (5%) commission, etc.);

(7) Daily and weekly hours of work;

(8) Total daily or weekly straight-time earnings;

(9) Total overtime excess compensation for the workweek, where applicable;

(10) Total additions to or deductions from wages paid each pay period;

(11) Total wages paid each pay period;

(12) Date of payment and the pay period covered by payment.

Q: Does an employer have to maintain all these records for exempt employees?

A: Employers must keep items (1) through (5) listed above, as well as the basis upon which the wages are paid in sufficient detail to permit calculation for each pay period of the employee's total remuneration for employment, including fringe benefits and perquisites.

14-2.   How Long to Keep Records

Q: How long must records be preserved?

A: The following represent some of those records which must be kept for three (3) years:

(1) Payroll records;

(2) Certificates, agreements, plans, notices, etc.;

(3) Sales and purchase records.

Some records which must be preserved for two (2) years are:

(1) Basic employment and earnings records;

(2) Wage rate tables;

(3) Worktime schedules;

(4) Order, shipping, and billing records;

(5) Records of additions to or deductions from wages paid;

(6) The basis for payment of any wage differential to employees of the opposite sex in the same establishment.

Q: Where must these records be kept?

A: They must be preserved in a safe and accessible place

where the employer's records are customarily maintained. They must be made available within seventy-two hours following notice from the Wage & Hour Division.

Q: Are there any special situations which must be documented or recorded?

A: Yes. In particular, all wage and hour information relevant to a *bona fide* collective bargaining agreement must be preserved. Also, records of employees paid overtime under any special overtime situations must be kept. Additionally, accurate records must be preserved on meal, lodging, and other facilities furnished to employees. Lastly, tip credit records must, of course, be maintained. See earlier discussion in Chapter 5.

Q: Must an employer make available to the Wage & Hour Compliance Officer any and all records?

A: Generally, the employer will probably have to show the Compliance Officer all relevant records which the employer is required to keep. However, one should contact the company attorney prior to revealing anything.

MAINTAIN ACCURATE RECORDS

15.

PENALTIES

15-1. Introduction

The criminal and civil penalties for violations of the Federal
Wage & Hour Law are severe. They are often cumulative, as well
as progressive. In other words, it is highly probable that investigations will occur more often, and penalties will be more costly,
as violations accumulate.

Aside from the specific statutory penalties, there are other
"penalties" frequently not considered, *e.g.,* the loss of administrative time and work time spent on the investigation, litigation
costs, morale problems, etc.

Policies found to be violative of the Wage & Hour Law sometimes foster corporate-wide investigations, resulting in lawsuits
seeking hundreds of thousands of dollars. Hence, be advised
that the penalties, tangible and intangible, are severe and sometimes devastating.

15-2. Criminal & Civil Penalties

Q: What are the penalties for Wage & Hour Law violations?

A: The following criminal and civil penalties are specifically authorized by the Law.

Criminal Penalties

Willful violations resulting in criminal convictions are subject to a fine of not more than $10,000 for *each count, offense, or violation,* or imprisonment for not more than six (6) months, or both, provided, however, no person shall be imprisoned unless it is his second conviction. This penalty has in fact been enforced. Employers have been recently convicted and sentenced.

Civil Penalties

Willful violations resulting in civil liability may require the employer to pay employees affected:

(1) All unpaid minimum wages;
(2) All unpaid overtime compensation;
(3) An additional equal amount as "liquidated damages";
(4) Reasonable attorneys' fees;
(5) Reinstatement; and
(6) Costs of the action.

Unintentional violations usually result in back wage payments only.

Additionally, the Wage & Hour Law authorizes the Federal District Court to issue an injunction to prevent future violations and insure compliance.

Child Labor violations are severely penalized as set forth in Chapter 9.

Q: If an employer fails to pay overtime after forty-six (46) hours, for example, does he have to pay back overtime pay after forty (40) hours?

A: The Wage & Hour Division has taken the position that hotels, motels, and restaurants are entitled to the favorable forty-six-hour (46) overtime treatment only when the employee is paid overtime after forty-six (46) hours. If an employer fails to pay overtime after forty-six (46) hours, the Wage & Hour Division argues that overtime pay is due after forty (40) hours. This position was dismissed by a Federal District Court which held that the employer was entitled to settle any unpaid overtime by paying time and one-half for all hours worked after forty-six (46), instead of after forty (40). However, this issue needs further adjudication by higher courts before one can be certain what a particular Area Director of the Wage & Hour Division will do.

15-3.   Statutes of Limitations

Q: What are the statutes of limitations on back wage recoveries?

A: Generally, there is a two-year statute of limitations for unintentional violations, and a three-year statute for willful offenses. The statute of limitations for equal pay violations is generally two (2) years. However, the statute of limitations for violations of the Age Discrimination in Employment Act is three (3) years.

Caveat: Any Wage & Hour Law violation can initiate an investigation of all wage policies, practices, and procedures.

Furthermore, a local investigation could trigger a corporate-wide investigation or lawsuit. The Solicitor of Labor has won the overwhelming majority of the lawsuits filed and has recovered millions of dollars in minimum wages, overtime pay, liquidated damages, equal pay, and age discrimination payments.

Recently, the Solicitor recovered over one million dollars from one employer. The time and expense of a Wage & Hour lawsuit is staggering. Hence, it is important to get your house in order before an investigator knocks on your door. The next section is devoted to a brief discussion of how to defend once the investigation has been instituted.

16.

DEFENSE BEGINS DURING THE WAGE & HOUR INVESTIGATION

16-1.   Introduction

The best defense is a corporate commitment to *preventive law* checkups, audits, surveys, and the like by competent professionals. The development of such a program is frequently stymied by attitudinal problems such as the "wait and see" approach which is called *reactive law* as opposed to *preventive law.*

A common practice is to wait for the tragedy, *i.e.,* the complaints and investigation, and then to react by defending, settling, and changing policies and practices to the extent required. This approach is the most expensive course of action, often guaranteeing regular investigations by the Wage & Hour Division.

If an investigation starts *before* an employer has conducted his or her own survey or audit, then one is always on the defensive.

However, since this is the situation in which most employers find themselves, this section discusses what to do when the Wage & Hour Division begins an investigation.

Q: Which hotels, motels, and restaurants will be investigated?

A: The Wage & Hour Division has over 1,200 Compliance Officers (investigators) in offices throughout the United States and Puerto Rico. These Compliance Officers cannot, of course, investigate each property covered by the Law. Generally, investigations reach less than five percent (5%) of those establishments covered. However, in spite of the small percentage of investigations, about 100 million dollars in unpaid minimum wages, overtime pay, Child Labor fines, equal pay, and age discrimination payments are recovered annually.

The Wage & Hour Division normally conducts investigations only after employee complaints have been lodged. Often a disgruntled employee, group of employees, or a labor union contacts the Wage & Hour Division, complaining that their Company is violating the Law.

More importantly, the Wage & Hour Division often discovers a general lack of compliance in a particular industry concerning whether and how the Law applies. Frequently this fact develops from investigations in a newly covered industry, such as hotels, motels, and restaurants. Therefore, the Wage & Hour Division may decide to conduct a general compliance review in the entire industry or to conduct spot investigations.

If an employer has been investigated in the past, it is likely there will be future checks.

16-2.   Notice

Q: **How much notice do employers have prior to an investigation?**

A: Sometimes the Wage & Hour Division gives several days notice. On the other hand, the Law does not require any notice prior to an investigation.

The instant an employer has knowledge of an impending investigation, counsel should be contacted. Most employers place themselves in a much more unfavorable (and expensive) position when they attempt to deal directly with the Compliance Officer.

Q: **Is it not true that most employers are to some extent violating the Wage & Hour Law?**

A: Because many of the traditions and established practices of paying employees in the hospitality and foodservice
industries run afoul of the requirements of the Wage & Hour
Law, the overwhelming majority of hotels, motels, and restaurants are to some extent violating the law, albeit unintentionally.
Most violations occur because of three failings:

(1) The employer is unfamiliar with the practical requirements of the law;
(2) The employer is unfamiliar with the duties actually performed by the
    employees; and
(3) The employer is unfamiliar with the hours actually worked by employ-
    ees.

For example, many employers believe that an office employee
spends most of his or her time doing exempt work, when in fact
he or she is nothing more than a clerk or bookkeeper.

As was pointed out above, a common violation is the determination of hours actually worked by employees. An employer
might believe that employees work an 8-to-5 shift with a half
hour for lunch during a forty hour (40) workweek. However,
the employee might report fifteen minutes early every day and
take only fifteen minutes for lunch. A simple calculation dem-
onstrates that the employee is probably entitled to overtime
compensation for a period of two and one-half hours per week.
If the facility has 100 employees in this situation paid $3.00 per
hour, the potential unpaid overtime liability for one year would
be approximately $56,250.000. This is computed as follows:

$$\$4.50 \text{ OT Rate} \times 2\tfrac{1}{2} \text{ Hrs. OT}$$
$$\text{per employee} \times 100 \text{ employees}$$
$$\times 50 \text{ weeks} = \$56,250.00$$

Periodic audits should be conducted to avoid such potential
liability. Furthermore, there should also be regular audits to
check for equal pay and age discrimination violations.

16-3.   Compliance Officers & Specialists

Q: What are Wage & Hour Compliance Officers like?

A: Wage & Hour Compliance Officers are usually much more friendly and professional than many of the government investigators with which employers come in contact. Accordingly, since employers often find these investigators so much more palatable than they imagined, they often overreact to the investigator's advantage and make costly good-faith admissions. Later, moreover, the employer is floored with a final determination seeking astronomical amounts of back wages.

Employers should be well advised that as a general rule the investigator is not normally inclined towards the employer. Additionally, most investigators investigate with a view towards finding violations. Since most establishments are violating the Law, the investigator is even more encouraged to look for violations.

Caveat: The Wage & Hour Division interprets the law for investigative purposes, but sometimes these interpretations are not supported by the courts.

Q: How should employers treat the Wage & Hour Compliance Officer?

A: Naturally, employers should exhibit reasonable and professional courtesy at all times. The Wage & Hour Compliance Officer should be convinced that the establishment has nothing to hide and will fully cooperate. Bear in mind, however, that employers are not bound to volunteer any information. All information should be furnished pursuant to a specific request by the investigator only.

16-4.   The Investigation

Q: What can the Wage & Hour investigation cover?

A: Although the Wage & Hour investigation may have been fostered by an individual age discrimination complaint, for example, the authority of the Wage & Hour Compliance Officer to conduct a broad compliance review of the entire hotel, motel, or restaurant is well established. Therefore, it is often very difficult to limit the scope of the investigation.

However, the investigator is only entitled to examine relevant data. The Secretary of Labor has broad subpoena powers to enforce compliance with a request by an investigator to inspect an employer's relevant books and records. Accordingly, an employer should deliver records and books to an investigator only after consulting an attorney.

Q: What does the investigator usually review?

A: Wage & Hour Compliance Officers review the relevant payroll data first. Employers should provide a separate room for the investigator, isolated from the majority of employees. Employers should keep records of every document delivered to the Wage & Hour investigator. Additionally, a record of which employees are interviewed on company time should be maintained.

Since overtime violations are so common, the investigator will often review the hourly payroll to determine whether overtime is being properly computed. The investigator, of course, checks whether the employee is actually compensated for hours actually worked. Secondly, the investigator determines whether the actual hours worked are in fact reported.

In many cases, employees arbitrarily record their time, either because they do it on their own or they are ordered to report the same number of hours each day or each week, regardless of the number of hours actually worked.

When an investigator examines timecards or time sheets, he will document the names of those employees whose recorded hours appear to be falsified or incorrect. The Compliance Officer will often select at random the names of certain hourly employees to interview concerning all wage practices. This is particularly true of those employees treated as exempt employees by the mangement.

Q: How should employers cooperate with employee interviews?

A: Although the employer can demand that the investigator interview all employees during non-working hours, it is generally to the employer's advantage to be able to monitor who is interviewed and when. Furthermore, this enables the company to document its cooperation. Employer cooperation during an investigation may be helpful in preventing an injunction suit in the event an agreement is not reached.

The employer should require the investigator to provide a list of all employees to be interviewed. Even though the employer does not have the right to be present during the interviews, the company does have the right to schedule the interviews in a manner which will least disrupt its operations.

Obviously, employees should be instructed to tell the truth. All employees should be informed of the basis for this interview, that the Wage & Hour Division is investigating possible violations of the Wage & Hour Law.

To expedite the investigation, it is sometimes desirable to ask all exempt employees to prepare personalized, tailored job descriptions. If these support the employer's position with respect to the exempt status of certain employees, then there may be no need for the Wage & Hour Compliance Officer to interview these employees.

All employees should be informed that they do not have to sign any statement prepared by the investigator. If they decide to sign the statement, they should read it carefully and ask for a copy. The Wage & Hour Division will not furnish copies of any employee statements to the employer.

Q: What happens after the completion of the investigation?

A: The Wage & Hour Compliance Officer will have a conference with management to discuss the preliminary findings of the investigation. At this stage, the employer may furnish any facts which are helpful to its position, if advisable.

In some cases, it is preferable to attempt to pinpoint the unfavorable conclusions of the investigator without furnishing the employer's most favorable evidence.

However, clear errors of law and fact should be rectified during this conference. Generally, the company should defer specific positions on the alleged violations until it submits its formal position statement. Sometimes the Wage & Hour investigator will compute a general estimate or summary of unpaid wages.

16-5.   Employer's Position Statement

Q: What is a Wage & Hour Position Statement?

A: Shortly after the first formal post-investigation conference, the employer's counsel should prepare a position letter to the Area Director for incorporation in the record of the investigation. This letter will document in detail the factual and legal position of the employer on each particular point.

If there are numerous technical points to be discussed, the company can, of course, submit various position letters. It is desirable to do this in the case of many violations, particularly where some are favorable, unfavorable, and in doubt.

Q: What is the next step in this administrative process?

A: Factual errors should be presented to the investigator's superior. Further negotiations with the higher administrative officials should be pursued with a view towards limiting liability and settling the case to avoid expensive litigation costs.

These negotiations can be pursued through the administrative hierarchy to the Regional Director of the Wage & Hour Division. If the matter is not resolved, it is normally referred to the Regional Office of the Solicitor of Labor for possible litigation. Should an employer administratively settle pending Wage & Hour Cases, it is recommended that each check for back wages be stamped on the back with following language:

NOTICE: Acceptance of this check acknowledges receipt of payment in full of any alleged unpaid wages due and means you have given up any right to sue under §16(b), Fair Labor Standards Act and Wage & Hour Laws, providing a right to sue for unpaid minimum wages and overtime pay, liquidated damages, attorney's fee, court costs, and releases your employer from any claims under Wage & Hour Laws as of this date.

Date _____

Signature _____

16-6.   Government Remedies

Q: What remedies does the Solicitor of Labor have to enforce a Wage & Hour Division determination that the law has been violated?

A: The Solicitor of Labor may file a complaint in Federal District Court for an injunction requesting that the employer be required to pay all back wages, overtime, etc. It is generally recognized that if the employer has retained counsel early in the case, settlement with an attorney from the Regional Solicitor's office will normally be for less than with the investigator.

There are two other available enforcement remedies of which employers should be aware. If settlement is not reached with the Wage & Hour Division, letters will be sent to each of the employees indicating the back wages owed them. The letter informs the employee of the right to retain an attorney to sue the employer for back wages plus an additional equal amount as liquidated damages plus attorneys' fees and costs, or, that the Wage & Hour Division will institute the suit for only the amount of the back wages purportedly owed if it is authorized to do so in writing.

It is obvious that terminated employees are more likely to sue than any other class of employees. Similarly, where there has been a high degree of turnover, these lawsuits are more common. Therefore, it is incumbent upon the employer to terminate an employee very carefully and after an accurately documented case of the employee's failings. *A fortiori* since the turnover is much higher in the hospitality and foodservice industries than in many others, employers must be particularly cognizant of the potential liability. If the "wait and see" approach is adopted rather than the *Preventive Law* method, problems necessarily develop.

16-7.   Union Effect

Q: Does the presence of a union foster or stymie Wage & Hour cases?

A: Since unions generally represent non-supervisory employees, the union's presence is normally irrelevant if questions are raised concerning the exempt status of employees. On the other hand, if the claim involves wage policies, practices, and procedures which are incorporated in the collective bargaining agreement or approved by the union through custom and practice, the union could be helpful to the company.

Furthermore, quite often employees will pursue their wage claims through a grievance procedure, rather than going to the Wage & Hour Division. If such is the case, the employer should take advantage of the opportunity to rectify Wage & Hour Law violations at that time. On the other hand, in many cases unions assist employees in maintaining class actions for back wages, liquidated damages, attorneys' fees, and costs. At any rate, the most important thing for the employer to do, whether his employees are union or non-union, is to institute a system of regular *preventive law* audits.

It cannot be overemphasized that all collective bargaining agreements should be "sanitized" from a Wage & Hour Law standpoint. It is very risky indeed to negotiate and implement a contract which contains clear Wage & Hour Law violations or even potential problem areas.

Since a collective bargaining agreement can be viewed as the subcontracting of a portion of one's personnel and wage administration departments, unions should recognize joint responsibility for certain kinds of Wage & Hour Law problems, *i.e.,* housemen/maids' equal pay questions.

17.

GARNISHMENTS*

17-1. Introduction

Roman Law decreed that forcing any person into court from his own house was unlawful, because a man's house was his sanctuary. If anyone lurked at home to avoid payment, he was summoned three times, with an interval of ten days between each summons, by the voice of a herald, by letters, or by the edict of a magistrate. If he still did not appear, the creditor was put in possession of the debtor's assets.

This procedure appears to be the basis of the custom of foreign attachment widely utilized in London in the eighteenth century. This custom provided a procedure for seizing assets of a nonresident debtor in the hands of a third person. Garnishment statutes enacted in the United States as early as the Colonial period were founded on the custom of attachment in London.

Despite this long history of garnishment laws, many court decisions in the United States in this century have created more rights for the individual whose paycheck is to be garnished.

The recession and spiraling inflation of the 1970s have resulted in a large increase in the number of garnishments filed. The creditor should be aware of the rights he has by this procedure, and he should remember that laws vary greatly among the

*Some of the material in this Chapter on Garnishments is reprinted from *The Seller's Credit Guide,* with permission of the authors, Marion B. Stokes, III, and Wayne H. Lazarus.

states. In Florida, for example, wages of the head of a house-hold cannot be garnished. Some states have no garnishment at all.

This chapter includes information on answering garnishments. Many creditors and sellers not only file garnishments, but they are also frequently served by garnishment summonses which must be answered.

The Wage & Hour Division administers, regulates, and enforces Title III of the Consumer Credit Protection Act, commonly called the Federal Wage Garnishment Law, effective July 1, 1970.

17-2. Definition

Q: What is a garnishment?

A: Garnishment is a legal proceeding by which a creditor may seize money which is owed to a debtor.

Example: A debtor has $5,000 on deposit in a bank. This means that the bank owes the debtor $5,000. The creditor cannot levy on this money because it is not in the debtor's pos-session, and the debtor's right to draw it out of the bank is intangible. As a recourse, the creditor can file a garnishment action which in this case, is an action in court against the debtor and the bank. The sheriff or marshal of the court delivers the summons of garnishment to the bank as garnishee. The bank must hold the money which the debtor has on deposit and pay it into the court for the benefit of the creditor. The money is then disbursed to the creditor by the court.

Recently, garnishment proceedings have been subject to attack in the courts. In general, the courts have held that the debtor must have notice of the garnishment, even after a judgment has been obtained. This means that the marshal or sheriff must deliver to the debtor a copy of the summons of garnishment, or the debtor must receive some notification of the garnishment action.

Q: What is a garnishment on suit pending?

A: A garnishment on suit pending is a garnishment which is filed at the same time as a lawsuit.

The United States Supreme Court has held that *wage* garnishments are not permitted until a judgment has been obtained. The Court has held that seizing wages prior to a trial on the suit constitutes the taking of property without due process of law, which violates the Fourteenth Amendment of the United States Constitution.

Some states allow garnishments, other than wage garnishments, to be filed on suit pending. For example, some states allow for a garnishment to issue to a debtor's bank account at the same time a suit is filed.

Caveat: Several courts have held that the filing of a garnishment of any kind prior to obtaining a judgment constitutes a violation of due process and is unconstitutional. Due process, in this instance, normally means a hearing.

Care should be taken in instituting any action prior to judgment, even though the law of the particular State may allow the garnishment or other action. In this developing area, the trend appears to be that a creditor's remedy prior to judgment will be severely restricted, but that in certain limited instances, the courts may allow the issuance of a prejudgment garnishment.

17-3.   Failure to Answer

Q: What if the garnishee fails to answer garnishment?

A: A judgment will be taken against the garnishee.

Example: A creditor has a judgment against a cook employed in a hotel. The creditor garnishes the hotel. The hotel does not answer, and the creditor enters judgment against the hotel. Now the creditor *can collect from the hotel.* He has the right to levy on the hotel's assets, garnish the hotel's bank account, and otherwise proceed to collect.

Garnishment Laws do allow for judgments against garnishees to be set aside within certain time periods, but this should be done by an attorney. In addition to attorneys' fees, the garnishee will be liable for at least the money he owed debtor or fifteen percent (15%) of the judgment, whichever is *greater.*

If you are regularly served with garnishments, have an established procedure for processing them so that money from the employee (or other person to whom the money is owed) will be withheld and the garnishment answered on time. If garnishments are received infrequently, consult commercial counsel so that the answer will be properly made and filed.

Q: What Laws restrict wage garnishments?

A: The Federal Wage Garnishment Law is Title III of the Consumer Credit Protection Act, which became effective July 1, 1970. It limits the amount of an employee's disposable earnings which may be garnished in any one week and prohibits discharge because of garnishment for any one indebtedness.

The law does not alter other matters related to garnishment, such as a creditor's right to collect the full debt, most State garnishment procedures, or the priority of garnishment orders when more than one is served on the employer. The Federal Wage Garnishment Law is enforced by the Wage & Hour Division.

Q: What wages are subject to garnishment?

A: The Law's restrictions on garnishment are based on the employee's disposable earnings, which are different from gross pay or take-home pay.

Q: What does the term "earnings" mean?

A: The term "earnings" means compensation paid or payable for personal services, whether called wages, salary, commission, bonus, or otherwise and includes periodic payments pursuant to a pension or retirement program.

Dollar values of meals and lodging furnished employees are generally regarded as earnings. However, since tips do not normally pass through the hands of the employer, they usually cannot be garnished.

17-4.   Disposable Earnings

Q: What constitutes an employee's "disposable earnings"?

A: An employee's "disposable earnings" include those earnings remaining after the legal deductions.

Examples of Legal Deductions:

(1) Federal Income Tax Withholding deductions (determined by the number of exemptions);
(2) Federal Social Security Tax deductions;
(3) State and City Tax Withholding deductions;
(4) State Unemployment Insurance Taxes; and
(5) Deductions required under state employee's retirement systems.

Examples of Deductions Not Required by Law:

(1) Deductions to purchase savings bonds;
(2) Deductions for contributions to religious, charitable, or educational organizations;
(3) Deductions for union dues and union initiation fees;
(4) Deductions for health and welfare premiums, including company retirement programs;
(5) Deductions for board, lodging, or other facilities furnished to an employee by the employer;
(6) Deductions for the purchase of stock in the employer's corporation;
(7) Deductions pursuant to an assignment of earnings;
(8) Deductions to repay loans or payroll advancements made by the employer;
(9) Deductions for merchandise purchased from the employer; and
(10) Deductions pursuant to garnishment orders.

Q: What are the legal restrictions on the amount of wages that can be garnished?

A: The maximum part of the total disposable earnings subject to garnishment in any workweek may not exceed the lessor of:

(1) Twenty-five percent (25%) of the disposable earnings for that week; or
(2) The amount by which disposable earnings for that week exceeds thirty

(30) times the Federal minimum hourly wage in effect at the time earnings are payable.

Example 1—Disposable Earnings:

		Pay	Disposable Earnings
Earnings:		$100.00	
Deductions:			
Federal Income Tax	$10.00		$10.00
F.I.C.A. (Soc. Sec.)	6.00		6.00
State Income Tax	1.00		1.00
Health Insurance	3.00		
Credit Union	6.00		
Union Dues	3.00		
Total:	$29.00	$100.00	$83.00

Example 2—Amount Subject to Garnishment For Weekly Pay Period:

Disposable Earnings	$83.00
$83 X 25% =	20.75
$83 – (30 X 2.30) =	14.00
Amount Subject to Garnishment:	$14.00

Q: What are the formulas for the amount subject to garnishment for pay periods in excess of one week?

A: The Secretary of Labor's formulas to determine the amount subject to garnishment for pay periods in excess of one week are as follows:

Bi-weekly	2 X 30 X min. wage
Semi-monthly	2 1/6 X 30 X min. wage
Monthly	4 1/3 X 30 X min. wage

Example 3—Bi-Weekly Pay Period:

Disposable Earnings	$180.00
$180 X 25% =	45.00
$180 – (2 X 30 X 2.30) =	42.00
Amount Subject to Garnishment:	$ 42.00

Example 4—Semi-Monthly Pay Period:

Disposable Earnings	$180.00
$180 X 25% =	45.00
$180 – (2 1/6 X 30 X 2.30) =	38.50
Amount Subject to Garnishment	$ 38.50

Example 5—Monthly Pay Period:

Disposable Earnings	$360.00
$360 X 25% =	90.00
$360 – (4 1/3 X 30 X 2.30) =	61.00
Amount Subject to Garnishment:	61.00

Q: **What if an employee is paid on a daily basis and only works two or three days a week?**

A: It is not permissible to divide the maximum amount subject to garnishment on a per day basis. If, for example, an employee whose wage rate is $20.00 a day works only two days in a work-week, the week's earnings of $40.00 cannot be garnished in any amount because 30 X 2.30 is more than the employee's total earnings.

Q: **What if an employer turns over the weekly payroll to a bank, putting each employee's net earnings in a checking account established for the employee under the payroll system?**

A: The garnishment restrictions apply to these earnings, even though they are in a bank account and not in the employer's hands.

17-5.   Federal vs. State Laws

Q: **What is the effect of the Federal Wage Garnishment Law on State Laws?**

A: The Federal Wage Garnishment Law does not annul, alter, or exempt any person from complying with State Laws which prohibit garnishments or provide for more limited garnishments than are allowed under the Federal Law. Any provision of a State Law that subjects less of an individual's earnings to garnishment than does the Federal Law will be the one that is applied under a garnishment order. On the other hand, the Federal Law provision is applied, if it results in a smaller garnishment.

Example: Where State Law restricts garnishment to a class of individuals such as householders and results in a lesser amount subject to garnishment than under the Federal Law, State Law rather than the Federal restriction will be applicable. This rule applies even though the State Law in other respects imposes restrictions on garnishment less favorable than the Federal Law. As to those provisions, the State Law will be preempted by the Federal restrictions, and the maximum amount subject to garnishment will be determined by the Federal Law.

17-6.   Procedural Requirements

Q: Does Federal or State Law govern the procedural requirements for garnishment?

A: There are no procedures that must be followed under the Federal Law, such as filing an affidavit or an application for exemption, in order for the limitations on garnishments to apply. A requirement in a State Law that an employer or employee must affirmatively claim an exemption as a condition to receiving it, or any other procedural requirement of similar effect, may not be applied to defeat the Federal limitations.

Where a State restriction on garnishment is more favorable to the employee than under Federal Law, however, the State provision will be applicable even though its availability is conditional upon such a procedural requirement. In cases where the employer or employee fails to follow the procedure and thus loses a more favorable State Law provision, the Federal Law provisions will apply.

In some states, the entire amount due the employee when a garnishment order is received is impounded until certain procedural requirements are met. The Wage & Hour Division takes the position that such State provisions are pre-empted by the Federal Law and that the Law's restrictions apply to these withholdings.

The first notice an employer has of a wage garnishment is the service of a court summons. This summons requires the employer to file an answer in court within a stated period of time. The answer will set forth what amounts the employer owes the employee as of the date the employer's answer is filed in court. Therefore, the time period in which the answer is to be filed is critical. Failure to file a timely answer could result in substantial monetary loss to the employer. Moreover, the employer could find that a judgment has been entered against the employer for the full amount of the employee's debt.

Q: Is an employer subject to inspection by the Wage & Hour Division if the State Law strictly regulates garnishment?

A: The Secretary of Labor may exempt an employer from compliance with federal garnishment law, if that employer is complying with the applicable state law restricting garnishments *and* that state law is "substantially similar" to the Federal Law. Kentucky and Virginia are examples of State Laws found to be substantially similar to the Federal Law.

In the absence of a determination that the State's Garnishment Law is "substantially similar" to the Federal Law, any section or provision of the State Law that results in a smaller garnishment amount is to be applied. And, of course, vice versa.

17-7.   Employee Termination and Discipline

Q: Can employees be discharged for garnishments?

A: The Federal Law prohibits an employer from discharging any employee because his or her earnings have been subjected to garnishment for any one indebtedness. The term "one indebtedness" refers to a single debt, regardless of the number of levies made or the number of proceedings brought for its collection. A distinction is therefore made between a single debt and the garnishment proceedings brought to collect it.

If several creditors combine their debts in a single garnishment action, the total amount is considered as "one indebtedness". Similarly, if a creditor joins several debts in a court action and obtains a judgment and writ of garnishment, judgment would be considered a single indebtedness for the purposes of this Law.

The protection against discharges renews with each employer, since the new employer has not been a garnishee with respect to that employee. Also note that any garnishment fully executed before July 1, 1970, the effective date of the Law, is not counted as an indebtedness.

Example—Limits of Discharge Provisions: A discharge for a first-time garnishment, such as an attachment of wages under a tax lien, would be in violation of the Law. The same would be true of a court order requiring an employer to withhold an employee's wages for child support or alimony. In the case of tax liens, several levies to collect a single tax delinquency (or to collect several years' tax arrears that are combined into a single indebtedness) would be treated as one indebtedness. On the other hand, each specific court order for the payment of child support or alimony that is in arrears is considered as a separate indebtedness.

Q: Can an employer suspend an employee for an indefinite period of time because of garnishment?

A: Since the discharge provision prohibits firing, a suspension for an indefinite period of time, or a suspension of such length that the employee's return is unlikely, may well be considered as tantamount to firing, and thus considered a discharge within the meaning of the Law.

Q: What can employers do to discipline employees for garnishments?

A: Some employers have a rule that the employee will be given warnings for the first two garnishments and will be discharged for the third garnishment within a year. Where at least two of these actions relate to separate indebtedness, discharge would not be prohibited by the Law, since the warning and discharge would be based on garnishments for more than one debt.

In some cases employers have established plans which prescribe disciplinary actions for violations of company standards of conduct. For example, discharge results if the employee violates three of the standards within a year. One of the actions considered as a violation may be garnishment of wages. If only one of these violations relates to garnishment, discharge would be prohibited by Law, since the discharge would result from garnishment for only one indebtedness. In other words, regardless of the employer's disciplinary plan, no discharge may be based either wholly or in part on a first-time garnishment.

The Law does not prohibit discharge if there are garnishment proceedings pursuant to a second debt.

Q: When are an employee's earning "subjected to garnishment"?

A: An employee's earnings are "subjected to garnishment" for the purposes of the Law when the garnishee (employer) is bound to withhold earnings and would be liable to the judgment creditor if the employer disregards the court order. Therefore, if an employee, upon being advised that garnishment is contemplated, obtains a release from the garnishor (creditor) before the garnishment order is issued, the employee's earnings have not been "subjected to garnishment".

The Law does not expressly provide any time limitation between a first and second garnishment. Where a considerable time has elapsed between garnishment (such as a year), it may be that the employee is actually being discharged for the current indebtedness. The first indebtedness may no longer be a material consideration in the discharge. Determinations in such cases will be made on an *ad hoc* basis.

18.

CONCLUSION

The Wage & Hour Law is very complicated in interpretation and in application, particularly to newly-covered industries. Accordingly, violations are common. More importantly, recent developments relevant to hospitality and foodservice facilities have caught many employers by surprise. Many wage practices, policies, and procedures traditional to hotels, motels, and restaurants are possibly violative of the Law and must be analyzed anew.

Furthermore, one must recognize that the Wage & Hour Law is dynamic; constantly being interpreted by the Wage & Hour Division, the Federal Courts, and the numerous State Wage & Hour Law agencies. Therefore, there are many exceptions to the general rules, and each problem has to be examined on an *ad hoc* basis.

Due to a much more active role in Wage & Hour Law regulation on the part of State agencies, it is crucial to familiarize oneself with the administrative agency enforcing and regulating the State Wage & Hour Law relevant to your hotel, motel, restaurant, or foodservice institution.

Generally, employers may be able to reduce their potential liability under Federal and State Wage & Hour Laws by following these basic rules:

BECOME ACQUAINTED WITH THE BASICS OF THE LAW

**INSURE THAT ALL EMPLOYEES ARE ACCURATELY PAID
FOR ALL HOURS WORKED**

**MAINTAIN PRECISE RECORDS OF ALL WAGE
POLICIES, PRACTICES, AND PROCEDURES**

CONDUCT REGULAR AUDITS AND CHECKUPS

Appendices

APPENDIX A

FEDERAL
WAGE & HOUR LAW
POSTERS
AND
DOCUMENTS

Attention Employees

Your Rights Under the Fair Labor Standards Act (Federal Wage and Hour Law)

The Act Requires . . .

Minimum Wage*

of at least:

$2.65 per hour

Beg. 1/1/79 - $2.90/hr.
Beg. 1/1/80 - $3.10/hr.
Beg. 1/1/81 - $3.35/hr.

beginning January 1, 1978

This minimum wage applies to workers engaged in or producing goods for interstate commerce or employed in certain enterprises.

Overtime Pay

at least 1-1/2 times your regular rate of pay for all hours worked over 40 in one workweek.

Equal Pay for Equal Work

regardless of sex.

Child Labor

You must be at least 16 years old to work in most nonfarm jobs; at least 18 to work in nonfarm jobs declared hazardous by the Secretary of Labor. Youths 14 and 15 may work in various jobs outside school hours under certain conditions. Different rules apply to agricultural employment.

Note: The act contains exemptions from the minimum wage and/or overtime pay requirements for certain occupations or establishments.

*Certain full-time students, student learners, apprentices, and handicapped workers may be paid less than the applicable minimum but only under special Department issued certificates.

Enforcement:

The U.S. Government may bring civil or criminal action against employers who violate the act. In certain actions, courts may order payment of back wages. Employers may be fined up to $1,000 for each violation of the child labor provisions. The act prohibits an employer from discriminating against or discharging you if you file a complaint or participate in a proceeding under it.

State laws:

When a state law differs with the Fair Labor Standards Act, the law providing more protection or setting the higher standard applies.

Additional information:

Consult your telephone directory under U.S. Government, Department of Labor.

or write:

U.S. Department of Labor
Employment Standards Administration
Wage and Hour Division
200 Constitution Avenue, N.W.
Washington, D.C. 20210

U.S. Department of Labor
Employment Standards Administration
Wage and Hour Division
200 Constitution Avenue, N.W.
Washington, D.C. 20210

The law requires employers to display this poster where employees can readily see it.

WH Publication 1088
Rev. January 1978

● U. S. GOVERNMENT PRINTING OFFICE : 1977 O - 253-094

U.S. DEPARTMENT OF LABOR
EMPLOYMENT STANDARDS ADMINISTRATION
Wage and Hour Division
675 Milner Building, 210 S. Lamar St.
Jackson, Mississippi 39201

Form Approved
Budget Bureau No. 44 R.15 x

APPLICATION FOR FEDERAL CERTIFICATE OF AGE

IMPORTANT: COMPLETE THIS FORM CAREFULLY. PRINT OR WRITE PLAINLY. A FEDERAL CERTIFICATE OF AGE CANNOT BE ISSUED WITHOUT APPROPRIATE DOCUMENTARY PROOF OF AGE. (SEE INSTRUCTIONS ON REVERSE SIDE.)

1. Name (First, middle, last)	2. Age	3. Sex

4. Present address (Number, street, P.O. box)

(City or town, county, state, zip code)

5. Place of birth (City, county, state)	6. Date of birth (Month, day, year)

7. Father's full name	8. Mother's full name (before marriage)

9. Name as shown on any previous age certificate	10. Are you applying for an age certificate to work in agriculture? ☐ Yes ☐ No

11. Check type of proof of age ATTACHED to this application (See instructions-reverse side). YOUR PROOF OF AGE WILL BE RETURNED TO YOU.

☐ Birth Certificate   ☐ Baptismal Certificate   ☐ Life Insurance Policy at least 1 year old   ☐ Passport

12. If for any reason, other than marriage, your last name as shown on this application is not the same as that shown on the documentary proof of date of birth attached to this application, please indicate when your name was changed and where this change is recorded (i.e. court records, school records, etc.)

13. Signature of minor submitting application

INTENTION TO EMPLOY PORTION

TO BE COMPLETED BY EMPLOYER IF: Applicant is under 18 years of age and to be employed in industry, or under 16 years of age and to be employed in agriculture.

The undersigned intends to employ the above named minor immediately upon receipt of a certificate showing that he is above the oppressive child-labor age for the occupation specified below, as defined by the Fair Labor Standards Act of 1938, as amended, and subsequent regulations:

14. Specific occupation of minor to be employed	15. Industry (such as retail, wholesale, mfg.)

16. Name of employer (company)

17. Business address of employer (Number, street, city, state, and zip code)

18. Daily and weekly hours minor is to be employed (if minor is under 16 years of age)	19. Is this employment subject to the Walsh-Healey Public Contracts Act? ☐ Yes ☐ No

20. Signature of employer or authorized representative	21. Date

Form WH 14 (Rev

INSTRUCTIONS

A FEDERAL CERTIFICATE OF AGE CANNOT BE ISSUED WITHOUT APPROPRIATE DOCUMENTARY PROOF OF AGE. THE PROOF OF AGE THAT YOU SUBMIT WILL BE RETURNED TO YOU.

1. Attach your birth certificate to this form.

   If you do not have a birth certificate you may:

   a. Obtain one from the Bureau of Vital Statistics in the State where you were born,

   b. Or (if unable to obtain a birth certificate) attach a copy of an official document which shows your full name, date (month/day/year) and place of birth, and parents' names, such as,

      — A baptismal certificate

      — A life insurance policy at least one year old

      — A passport.

2. Return the completed form with the documentary proof of age to the address shown at the top of this form.

If the information that you give is complete, the documentary proof of your age is satisfactory, and the job you are to do is permissible for a person of your age, the certificate will be mailed to your employer, and you will receive a notice that it has been issued. If you are 18 years or over the certificate will be given to you if you apply in person or will be mailed to you unless the employer requests otherwise. If you are 16 years of age and to be employed in agriculture, the certificate will be mailed to you.

GPO 879 470

Persons 40-65 Years Note!

The Federal Age Discrimination in Employment Act prohibits arbitrary age discrimination in employment by:

- Private Employers of 20 or more persons
- Federal, State, and Local Governments, without regard to the number of employees in the employing unit
- Employment Agencies serving such employers
- Labor Organizations with 25 or more members

Certain exceptions are provided.

If you feel you have been discriminated against because of age, contact the nearest office of the Wage and Hour Division, U. S. Department of Labor. It is important to contact the Division promptly.

If you wish to bring a court action yourself, you must first notify the Secretary of Labor of your intent to do so. This notice should be filed promptly, but in no event later than *180* days after the alleged unlawful practice occurred.

Questions on State age discrimination laws should be directed to State authorities. These laws may affect the *180* day time limit noted above.

Questions on Federal employment should be directed to the U. S. Civil Service Commission, Washington, D. C. 20415.

U. S. Department of Labor
Employment Standards Administration
Wage and Hour Division

WH Publication 1289 (Rev. 5/76)   ☆ U.S. GOVERNMENT PRINTING OFFICE: 1976 O--207-995

NOTE: As of 1979 the Age Discrimination Act protects those aged **40-70** years.

Control No.

U. S. DEPARTMENT OF LABOR Employment Standards Administration Wage and Hour Division	CHILD LABOR CIVIL MONEY PENALTY REPORT - NONAGRICULTURE
Name of Employer	Region
Location	SIC Code

		Minors Illegally Employed							
A. ILLEGAL EMPLOYMENT IN NONAGRICULTURE (Enter designated amount for each violation for each minor)									
1. No proof of age	$ 50.								
2. Reg. 3 standards for 14/15-year-old									
Occupation	$100.								
Hours/Time Standards	$100.								
12- or 13-year-olds	$300.								
Under 12 years old	$500.								
3. Hazardous Occupations Orders									
16- or 17-year-old	$250.								
Under 16 years old	$500.								
4. Recurring or willful child labor violations	$500.								
5. Serious injury sustained while engaged in illegal employment	$500.								
6. Permanent total or partial disability or death resulting from illegal employment * Secs. B,C,D inapplicable. This assessment is never reduced.	$1000. *								
Subtotal →									
B. Subtotal A would be reduced by 50% if neither of the following is present: 1. Recurring or willful child labor violations. 2. Serious injury while illegally employed.									
Subtotal →									
C. Subtotal B would be reduced 20% in establishments or enterprises (when applicable) employing less than 100 employees.									
Subtotal →									
D. No penalty to be assessed if all of the following conditions are present: 1. Full child labor compliance achieved. 2. Future child labor compliance assured. 3. No aggravated child labor violations. 4. Child labor violations were neither willful nor recurring. 5. No serious injury while illegally employed. 6. Total number of minors in violation does not exceed four (4). (Maximum $1,000 per Minor)									
Total Assessed Penalty →									

Compliance Officer	Date (Mo., day, year)

Form WH-265
July 1975

RECEIPT FOR PAYMENT OF BACK WAGES

As computed or approved by the Wage and Hour Division
Employment Standards Administration
U. S. Department of Labor

Form Approved.
Budget Bureau No. 44—R0343

I,_____, hereby acknowledge receipt of payment in full
      (Type or print name of employee)

from_____
                              (Name and location of establishment)

for the period beginning with the workweek ending_____through the workweek

ending_____of unpaid wages due me (as shown in the column to the right) under

the Act(s) indicated in the marked box(es):   ☐   The Davis-Bacon and
                                                  Related Acts

☐   The Fair Labor Standards Act   ☐   The Contract Work Hours
                                          Standards Act   Gross amount $_____

☐   The Walsh-Healey   ☐   The Age Discrimination
    Public Contracts Act   in Employment Act   Legal deductions $_____

☐   The Service Contract Act   ☐   Title III - Consumer
                                          Credit Protection Act   Net amount received $_____

NOTICE TO EMPLOYEE.—Your acceptance of back wages due under the *Fair Labor Standards Act* means that you have given
up any right you may have to bring suit for such back wages under Section 16(b) of that Act. Section 16(b) provides that an
employee may bring suit on his own behalf for unpaid minimum wages and/or overtime compensation and an equal amount
as liquidated damages, plus attorney's fees and court costs. Generally, a 2-year statute of limitations applies to the recovery
of back wages. Do not sign this receipt unless you have actually received payment of the back wages due.

Signature of employee_____

Date_____   Address_____
                                               (Number, Street, (Apt. No.), City, State, ZIP Code)

EMPLOYER'S CERTIFICATION

To Wage and Hour Division, Employment Standards Administration, U. S. Department of Labor

I hereby certify that I have on this (date)_____paid the above-named employee
in full covering unpaid wages as stated above.

Signed_____   Title_____
        (Employer or authorized representative)

PENALTIES ARE PRESCRIBED FOR FALSE STATEMENTS AND FALSE RECEIPTS

1. WAGE AND HOUR COPY   Form WH—58 (Rev. 6/71)

Tipped Employees Under the Fair Labor Standards Act

U.S. Department of Labor
Employment Standards Administration
Wage and Hour Division

WH Publication 1433
(Issued January 1978)

Tips actually received by tipped employees may be counted as wages for
purposes of the Act in an amount up to 50 percent of the applicable
minimum wage. The Act requires that (1) the employer must inform
tipped employees about this tip credit allowance before the credit is
utilized; (2) the employees must be allowed to retain all tips (individually or through a pooling arrangement) and this is so regardless of
whether the employer elects to take a credit for tips received; and
(3) the employer must be able to show that the employee receives at least
the minimum wage in the combination of direct wages and the tip credit.
In other words, employers must pay tipped employees at least half of the
applicable minimum wage (from their own pockets) for each hour worked
and may take a tip credit of no more than 50 percent of the required
minimum wage. The tip credit that an employer may take is reduced from
50 percent of the applicable minimum wage to 45 percent effective
January 1, 1979, and further reduced to 40 percent effective January 1,
1980.

For hotel, motel, and restaurant employees who are subject to the Act,
the current minimum wage is $2.65 an hour increasing to $2.90 an hour
effective January 1, 1979; to $3.10 an hour effective January 1, 1980; and
to $3.35 an hour effective January 1, 1981. Accordingly, the maximum
tip credit that may be taken will be as follows:

	Minimum Wage	Maximum Tip Credit	Cash Wage
Effective January 1, 1978	$2.65	$1.32 - (50%)	$1.33
Effective January 1, 1979	$2.90	$1.30 - (45%)	$1.60
Effective January 1, 1980	$3.10	$1.24 - (40%)	$1.86
Effective January 1, 1981	$3.35	$1.34 - (40%)	$2.01

Hotel or motel employees who perform maid or custodial services must be
paid not less than time and one-half their regular rates of pay for hours
worked in excess of 40 per week. Employees of hotels, motels, and restaurants who are not otherwise exempt (other than maids or custodial
employees) must be paid not less than time and one-half their regular
rates of pay for hours worked in excess of 44 hours per week effective
January 1, 1978, and effective January 1, 1979, after 40 hours per week.

A "tipped employee" is any employee engaged in an occupation in which he or she customarily and regularly receives more than $30 a month in tips. Tips may include amounts designated as a "tip" by credit card customers on their charge slips. Where tips are charged on a credit card and the employer must pay the credit card company a percentage of the bill for the use of its credit facilities, a practice whereby the employer reduces the amount of credit card tips paid over to the employee by an amount no greater than that charged by the credit card company will not be questioned. However, this will not be permitted where it reduces the employee's wage below the required minimum wage. Moreover, the amount due the employee must be paid no later than the regular pay day and may not be held while the employer is awaiting reimbursement. The law forbids any arrangement whereby any part of the tips of a tipped employee belong to the employer or are retained by the employer. Under the Act, a tip becomes the property of the tipped employee in recognition of whose service it is presented by the customer.

The requirement that an employee must retain all tips does not preclude tip splitting or pooling arrangements among employees who customarily and regularly receive tips, such as waiters, bellhops, waitresses, countermen, busboys, and service bartenders. It is not required that the particular busboys and others who share in tips must themselves receive tips from customers. Both the amounts retained by the waiters and those given the busboys are considered the tips of the individuals who retain them. Employees who share in tips are tipped employees if they receive more than $30 a month in tips from the pool.

Tipped employees may not be required to share their tips with employees who have not customarily and regularly participated in tip pooling arrangements, such as dishwashers, chefs, and janitors. Also, waiters and waitresses cannot be required to contribute a greater percentage of their tips than is customary and reasonable. Only those tips that are in excess of tips used for the tip credit, i. e., those in excess of half the minimum wage, may be taken for a pool.

To calculate the tips an employee receives per hour, divide total tips for the week by the hours worked that week. If a waitress or waiter, for example, (where the applicable minimum wage is $2.65 per hour) works 40 hours and receives $40 in tips in a week, the tips average $1 an hour. The employer must pay $1.65 an hour to the employee ($2.65 minus $1) or $66 more for the week, making the total received $106 for that week. The same method of computation is used whenever a change in the minimum wage occurs.

NOTE: An employer may not take a greater tip credit in overtime hours than he does in straighttime hours.

A compulsory charge for service, for example 15 percent of the bill, is not a tip. Such charges are part of the employer's gross receipts, and where service charges are imposed and the employees receive no tips, the employer must pay the entire minimum wage and overtime as required by the Act.

For further information, contact your local Wage and Hour Office, usually listed in telephone directories under U.S. Government, Department of Labor.

STATE WAGE & HOUR LAWS: A SUMMARY

The following summaries of each state's Wage & Hour Law are obviously for illustrative purposes and are effective as of January 1, 1978. Accordingly, you are encouraged to contact the relevant agency (addresses for which are listed alphabetically by state on pp. 156–163) in order to keep abreast of the many and frequent changes in the state laws, regulations, and applicable court decisions. Contact your local labor lawyer to insure compliance with all recent developments in the law.

ALABAMA WAGE & HOUR LAW

LAW. There is no relevant Minimum Wage Law in Alabama.

MINIMUM WAGE. No provision.

OVERTIME. No provision.

CREDITS. No provision.

CHILD LABOR LAW. No one under twenty-one (21) may serve alcoholic beverages for consumption on the premises, or in any poolroom or billiard room.

No one under eighteen (18) may work in that part of an establishment where alcoholic beverages are sold for consumption on the premises, except that minors sixteen (16) to eighteeen (18) may work as busboys/girls, dishwashers, janitors, etc. This Law is not applicable to members of the immediate family of the owner or operator, provided the employer keeps an age certificate on file for each employee age sixteen (16) or seventeen (17) and such minors do not sell, serve, dispense, or handle alcoholic beverages.

No one under sixteen (16) may work on the stage of any concert or theatrical exhibition (but may work as an usher and in concession stands), on scaffolding, in bowling alleys, in the operation of any motor vehicle, or in any place of occupation hazardous to life, limb, health, or morals.

The hours of minors are limited to eight (8) hours per day, forty (40) hours per week, and six (6) days per week when school is not in session; four (4) hours per day, twenty-eight (28) hours per week, and 7 a.m. to 8 p.m. when school is in session. No child under sixteen (16) may work during school hours, unless such child has completed high school.

ALASKA WAGE & HOUR LAW

LAW. Alaska's Wage & Hour Law covers all employees, except those under eighteen (18) employed on a part-time basis of not more than thirty (30) hours per week. Also exempt are administrative and professional personnel, outside salespeople, and salespeople on a straight commission.

The Commissioner of Labor may grant exemptions for learners, apprentices, and employees whose earning capacities are impaired by a physical or mental deficiency, an injury, or age.

MINIMUM WAGE. The minimum wage for hours worked in a pay period is set at $.50 greater than the prevailing Federal minimum wage or $2.60, whichever is greater, whether the work is measured by time, piece, commission, or otherwise.

OVERTIME. Time and one-half is provided for hours worked over eight (8) per day or forty per week. Overtime does not apply to employers with less than four (4) employees. Overtime does not apply to casual workers as defined by the Commissioner of Labor.

CREDITS. Tips may not be credited against the minimum hourly wage.

EQUAL PAY. No employer may discriminate in the payment of wages between the sexes or employ a female at a lower wage or salary than the rate paid to a man for comparable work.

Employers of women shall maintain records of the wages and wage rates, job classifications, and other terms and conditions of employment and make such reports as the Department of Labor prescribes.

Additionally, there are provisions for both civil and criminal enforcement.

CHILD LABOR LAW. The Alaska Child Labor Law exempts from coverage children under the direct supervision of a parent in a business owned and operated by the parent. Otherwise, children under fourteen (14) may be employed only in domestic work such as baby-sitting in private homes.

Minors fourteen (14) to sixteen (16) may work only outside school hours. When school is in session, they are limited to three (3) hours per day, eighteen (18) hours per week, and six (6) days per week. When school is not in session, they are limited to eight (8) hours per day and forty (40) hours per week. They may work only from 7 a.m. to 7 p.m., except June 1 to Labor Day from 7 a.m. to 9 p.m.

Children fourteen (14) to sixteen (16) may not work in restaurants, outside washing windows above ground, around power-driven kitchen or bakery equipment, in freezers or meat coolers, in nonclerical jobs in the transportation of persons or property, or use sharpened instruments. They may do office and clerical work, cashiering, selling, modeling, advertising, store clerking, clean-up work using vacuum cleaners and floor waxers, and ground maintenance not involving the use of power-driven mowers or cutters.

Minors under eighteen (18) may not work more than eight (8) hours per day, forty (40) hours per week, and six (6) days per week. They may not work in dangerous occupations exposing them to radiation; ride a freight elevator without an assigned operator; operate power-driven bakery machinery; work in and around laundry and dry cleaning plants; install, operate, or maintain electrical equipment over 220 volts; work in a poolroom or billiard room; or work in any industry where a strike or lockout is in progress.

Girls under eighteen (18) may not be employed as maids in hotels or lodging houses.

The Commissioner may grant exemptions for minors sixteen (16) to eighteen (18) during school vacations and for those who have graduated from high school, if he determines that the actual duties to be performed by the minors would not unduly endanger their lives, limbs, health, or morals.

No one under nineteen (19) may sell or serve intoxicating liquors or work in a room where intoxicating liquors are served for consumption on the premises, except that persons over eighteen (18) may be employed there as musicians, entertainers, or busboys/girls.

Employers must obtain a valid certificate of age to file for each employed minor and attach it to the application for exemption. An employer shall present the certificate of age to the minor on termination of his/her employment.

ARIZONA WAGE & HOUR LAW

LAW. Arizona's Minimum Wage Law applies only to minors under eighteen (18) and does not apply to a minor whose principal occupation is that of a student actually attending school.

MINIMUM WAGE. The Arizona procedure is to empower the Industrial Commission to investigate and set minimum wage rates in any industry where it finds that oppressive and unreasonable wages are being paid to minors. The Industrial Commission may allow a lower wage rate for minors who are learners, apprentices, and physically or mentally handicapped, than for experienced minors.

OVERTIME. No relevant provision.

CREDITS. No relevant provision.

EQUAL PAY. Arizona requires equal rates of pay for both sexes for work of the same quantity, quality, and classification.

CHILD LABOR LAW. No one under nineteen (19) may dispose of or sell spirituous liquors.

No one under eighteen (18) may operate power-driven bakery machines, elevators or power-driven hoist equipment, power-driven woodworking machines, work as a motor vehicle driver, or do work involving exposure to radiation.

No one under sixteen (16) may do any of the following types of work in a retail food or gasoline service establishment: outside window washing above ground level; cooking and baking, except at soda fountains, lunch counters, snack bars, and cafeteria serving counters; operating or maintaining power-driven food slicers, grinders, choppers, cutters, and bakery-type mixers; working in freezers and meat coolers; or loading and unloading trucks.

Children under sixteen (16) may not work in dressing poultry, filleting fish, cracking nuts, commercial laundering, operation or tending of hoisting apparatus or power-driven machinery, transportation of persons or property, warehousing and storage, or construction and repair.

Children under sixteen (16) may be employed only between 6 a.m. and 9:30 p.m. They may work no more than eight (8) hours per day and forty (40) hours per week when school is not in session; no more than three (3) hours per day and eighteen (18) hours per week when school is in session.

The Child Labor Law does not apply to minors who are employed under the supervision of a parent or guardian. It does not apply to performers or those minors involved in career education, vocational training, or apprenticeship programs.

ARKANSAS WAGE & HOUR LAW

LAW. Arkansas's Wage & Hour Law applies to employers with five (5) or more employees, except those covered by Federal Wage & Hour Law.

MINIMUM WAGE. The minimum wage rate is $2.00 per hour. Full-time students who are employed up to twenty (20) hours per week when school is in session, or up to forty (40) hours per week when school is not in session, may be paid not less than eighty-five percent (85%) of the minimum wage rate.

The Arkansas Labor Board may provide for lower minimum wage rates for learners, apprentices, and those whose earning capacities are impaired by a physical or mental deficiency, an injury, or age.

OVERTIME. Employees working in any mercantile establishment, hotel, restaurant, or eating place must be paid time and one-half for all hours worked over eight (8) per day and for work on the seventh consecutive day.

CREDITS. Tips actually received may be credited against the minimum wage up to $.90 per hour, provided that wages paid must be no less than $1.10 per hour in addition to tips.

Meals, lodging, apparel, and other items customarily and regularly furnished to the employee for his/her benefit may be credited against the minimum wage to the extent of their reasonable value in an amount not to exceed $.30 per hour.

EQUAL PAY. No female may be paid a salary or wage rate less than that paid to male employees for comparable work; however, reasonable variations in rates based on seniority, experience, training, skills, abilities, differences in duties and shifts, and any other reasonable differentiations, except sex, are permitted. Employees must be given a lunch break, a rest period in the first half of the workday, and a rest period in the last half of the workday.

CHILD LABOR LAW. No one under twenty-one (21) may mix or serve alcoholic beverages. Persons under eighteen (18) may be employed as musicians, and in foodservice and housekeeping, in establishments licensed to sell mixed drinks.

No one under eighteen (18) may work more than ten (10) hours per day, fifty-four (54) hours per week, and six (6) days per week. They may work only from 6 a.m. to 10 p.m., except later on nights preceding non-school days.

These restrictions do not apply to minors sixteen (16) to eighteen (18) who have graduated from high school, vocational or technical schools, or those who are married or are parents.

No one under sixteen (16) may work without an employment certificate, or work more than eight (8) hours per day, forty-eight (48) hours per week, and six (6) days per week. They may work only from 6 a.m. to 7 p.m., except until 9 p.m. on nights preceding non-school days.

Children under sixteen (16) may not work in any saloon, resort, or bar where intoxicating liquors are sold or dispensed; upon the stage of any theatre or concert hall or in connection with any theatrical performance or other exhibition or show; in any bowling alley; in any poolroom or billiard room; or in any occupation deemed dangerous to the child's life, limb, health, or morals.

Children under fourteen (14) may not be employed, except that they may be employed by their parents or guardians during school vacations. No child may be employed who has not passed four grades in school or the equivalent thereof.

CALIFORNIA WAGE & HOUR LAW

LAW. There is no statutory minimum wage in California, since all wage rates are set by wage orders.

MINIMUM WAGE. Wage Order 5-76 covers public housekeeping, including restaurants, clubs, hotels, motels, etc. The minimum wage is $2.50 per hour.

Learners and apprentices may be paid $2.15 an hour for the first 160 hours of employment.

Minors may be paid $2.15 per hour, provided that no more than twenty-five percent (25%) of the regular employees are minors paid at this rate, except that an employer with not more than ten (10) employees may employ three (3) minors at this rate. The twenty-five percent (25%) limitation does not apply during school vacations.

By special permit from the California Department of Labor, handicapped workers may be paid at a lower rate.

OVERTIME. Time and one-half is required for all hours worked over eight (8) per day or forty (40) per week and for the first eight (8) hours of work on the seventh consecutive day. Double time is required for hours over twelve (12) per day, and over eight (8) on the seventh consecutive day.

CREDITS. No tip credit is allowed in California.

Meals may be credited at $.90 for breakfast, $1.25 for lunch, and $1.65 for dinner.

No credit for uniforms or their maintenance may be taken, but a deposit may be required.

Where lodging is furnished by an employer, it may be credited up to $12.00 per week for a shared room, two-thirds of the rental value of an apartment not to exceed $140 per month, or $210.00 per month where a couple is employed by an employer.

An employer may not deduct for cash shortages, breakage, or equipment loss, unless such was the result of the employee's gross negligence, or dishonest and willful act.

EQUAL PAY. Equal pay for equal work is required.

CHILD LABOR LAW. Employers may not employ any person under twenty-one (21) years of age to work in that portion of an establishment where alcoholic beverages are sold or consumed.

Minors sixteen (16) and seventeen (17) employed by restaurants may not work more than eight (8) hours per day or forty-eight (48) hours per week. Minors sixteen (16) and seventeen (17) may not work before 5 a.m. or after 10 p.m. other than in certified work-experience programs. Minors sixteen (16) and seventeen (17) may not be employed more than four (4) hours per day on a school day. The 10 p.m. curfew does not apply to minors for nights preceding a non-school day; in such case, a minor may work until 12:30 a.m. preceding such non-school day.

The age of majority if eighteen (18) in California, and employment certificates are necessary for all minor workers.

If employers employ minors in more than twenty-five percent (25%) of their work force, all minors must be paid the adult rate of $2.50 per hour.

SPLIT SHIFT. An employee required to work a split shift must be paid $2.50 as a bonus for each day on which the split shift occurs, unless the employee resides at the place of employment.

COLORADO WAGE & HOUR LAW

LAW. Colorado's Wage & Hour Law generally covers only minors under eighteen (18) and women. Men are probably covered due to recent State and Federal developments prohibiting discrimination on the basis of sex.

MINIMUM WAGE. In cities with a 1960 population of 15,000 or more, the minimum rate is $1.10 per hour, $1.00 per hour with meals, and $.85 per hour with full maintenance, including room and board seven (7) days a week.

In other areas of the State, the minimum rate is $1.00 per hour, $.90 with meals, and $.75 with full maintenance.

For inexperienced employees with less than 200 hours of experience and for students under sixteen (16), the minimum rate may be $.20 less than the applicable minimum rate. For student learners under eighteen (18), the minimum rate may be $.15 less than the applicable minimum rate.

Handicapped workers may be paid at a lower rate with a special license.

OVERTIME. Overtime at the rate of time and one-half is required after a workweek of forty-two (42) hours for women and minors. Minors are to be paid the same rate as women for working more than eight (8) hours per day and forty-two (42) hours per week.

CREDITS. A tip credit may not be taken by the employer toward the minimum wage, unless the employer posts in a prominent place a sign 12 X 15 inches in size, with letters at least one-half inch high, declaring all tips to be the property of the employer. If such sign is posted, all tips and gratuities belong to the employer, and he must pay the minimum wage.

No uniform credits are allowed.

Meals must be provided free of charge to the employee if required by the job.

An employer may require employees to purchase and maintain ordinary white uniforms; provided, however, no special style, embroidery, or insignia is required by the employer.

No deduction may be taken for shortages or breakage, unless the employer shows that such was the result of a dishonest or negligent act of the employee.

EQUAL PAY. Equal pay, regardless of sex, is required for equivalent work.

CHILD LABOR LAW. No one under twenty-one (21) may sell or dispense spirituous liquors.

No one under eighteen (18) may sell or dispense malt or vinous liquors.

No one under sixteen (16) may be employed in the operation of a motor vehicle.

Except in emergencies, no one under sixteen (16) may be employed more than eight (8) hours per day, forty (40) hours per week, and more than six (6) hours on a day before a school day. No minor may be employed in a dangerous occupation, including work involving the risk of falling from an elevation of ten (10) feet or more, exposure to radiation, and operation of certain power-driven equipment.

Minors over fourteen (14) may operate elevators; perform janitorial work and clerical work; load and unload vehicles; work in retail food-service, restaurants, hotels, motels, etc. (except operation of power food slicers and grinders is prohibited); work in retail stores; carry out non-hazardous construction and repair work; and do work related to parks and recreation, etc.

Minors over twelve (12) may do gardening and lawn care, including the use of power-driven lawn equipment and snow-removal equipment; baby-sitting; etc.

Minors over nine (9) may shine shoes, caddie on golf courses, clean walks without power-driven equipment, and do gardening and lawn care without power-driven equipment.

Any minor fourteen (14) or fifteen (15) must obtain a school-release permit to work during school hours. These regulations do not apply to work done for a parent or guardian, or to models and performers, or to those granted an exemption for occupational training.

CONNECTICUT WAGE & HOUR LAW

LAW. All employees are protected, except those employees in camps and resorts open no more than six (6) months of the year, domestic servants in private homes, administrative and professional employees, etc. Restaurants and hotel restaurants are covered under State Wage & Hour Law regulations.

MINIMUM WAGE. Where the Federal Wage & Hour Law applies, the Connecticut minimum wage is one-half of one percent (1%) rounded higher to the nearest cent, e.g., if the Federal Wage & Hour Law is $2.90 an hour, the Connecticut minimum wage is $2.91.

Where the Federal Wage & Hour Law does not apply, the Connecticut minimum wage is $1.85 per hour.

Any restaurant employee regularly reporting for work, unless notified the previous day not to report, must be assured of not less than the minimum rate for four (4) hours' earnings.

For minors, learners, and apprentices, the minimum rate is $1.50 per hour for the first 200 hours of employment and $1.85 thereafter. Lower rates may also be set for the physically and mentally handicapped.

OVERTIME. For restaurant employees not covered by Federal Law, time and one-half for hours over forty-eight (48) per week and for all hours worked on the seventh consecutive day is required. Overtime is required at time and one-half for all hours in excess of forty (40) per week in restaurants covered by Federal Wage & Hour Law.

CREDITS. Tips for restaurant employees may be credited against the minimum wage to the extent of $.60 per hour, provided the employer keeps a separate weekly record of tips received, and the record is signed by the employee.

No credits against minimum wage are granted for uniforms furnished to the employee by the employer.

Wages may include an allowance for the reasonable value of lodging provided by the employer, up to $4.00 per week for a private room, or $3.00 per week for a room shared with others. Also, wages may include an allowance for meals up to $.60 for a full meal and $.35 for a light meal, provided that this does not exceed $1.80 per day for full meals and $.70 per day for light meals.

CHILD LABOR LAW. No one under eighteen (18) may be employed in any capacity in an establishment selling alcoholic beverages, except in premises operating under a package-store beer permit.

No one under eighteen (18) may work during the hours from 10 p.m. to 6 a.m., except those sixteen (16) to eighteen (18) may work to 12 midnight in restaurants if they do not have school the following day.

A minor sixteen (16) to eighteen (18) must have an age certificate from school officials to work in restaurants, theatrical establishments, bowling alleys, barbershops, etc.

No one under eighteen (18) may work in any hazardous occupation as defined by the Health Department or the Labor Department.

No one under sixteen (16) may work in restaurants, theatrical establishments, bowling alleys, barbershops, etc., except in an approved work-study or summer-work recreation program.

Minors under sixteen (16) may not operate an elevator or work on scaffolding, or where they are required to stand constantly.

No one under fourteen (14) may be employed in any capacity.

DELAWARE WAGE & HOUR LAW

LAW. Delaware's Minimum Wage Law covers all employees except supervisors.

MINIMUM WAGE. The rate is $2.00 per hour. Exceptions apply to learners, apprentices, and handicapped workers. Special rates for these classes are set by the Delaware Department of Labor.

OVERTIME. No provision.

CREDITS. Tips may be computed for employees regularly making more than $20.00 a month in tips, but only to fifty percent (50%) of the minimum wage. Other deductions are allowed only where required by Law, or authorized by the employee for his/her benefit.

CHILD LABOR LAW. No one under nineteen (19) may serve liquor in a restaurant.

No one under eighteen (18) may work in a restaurant where liquor is served or pilot a boat.

No one under sixteen (16) may work on a theatrical or concert stage, a boat, or on scaffolding; operate a passenger elevator, motor vehicle, or dangerous electrical machinery; or work in any occupation dangerous to the life, limb, health, or morals of the employee.

No one under fourteen (14) may be employed.

Minors may work only during the hours of 6 a.m. to 7 p.m., and no more than eight (8) hours per day, forty-eight (48) hours and six (6) days per week. They must have at least a thirty-minute (30) break between 11:30 a.m. and 2 p.m.

DISTRICT OF COLUMBIA WAGE & HOUR LAW

LAW. Federal Law governs within the District of Columbia, and all employees are covered under the District of Columbia's Wage & Hour Law, except supervisors and administrators. Wage Order No. 10 governs restaurants and allied occupations.

MINIMUM WAGE. The minimum rate for full-time workers is $3.25 per hour with automatic wage adjustments.

For part-time employees who work thirty (30) hours per week or less, the minimum rate is $2.93 per hour, or $2.61 if the employer is under rent control (except for minors and adult learners).

For adult learners and apprentices, the minimum rate is $2.50 per hour, or $2.22 if the employer is under rent control.

For minors under eighteen (18), the rate is $2.25 per hour, or $2.00 if the employer is under rent control.

Reduced wage rates for handicapped workers may be authorized by the Minimum Wage and Industrial Safety Board.

When an employee reports to work at his regular schedule, he/she must be paid for at least four (4) hours of work, even if sent home and given no work.

When an employee is required to work a split shift, or when the beginning and end of the workday are more than ten (10) hours apart, the employee must be paid an additional $2.80 per day, or $2.50 if the employer is under rent control.

OVERTIME. Time and one-half is the overtime rate for over forty (40) hours, unless the employee's regular rate of pay is at least one and one-half times the minimum rate.

For four (4) hours of work, the employer may provide and deduct no more than $1.10 for no more than one (1) meal furnished. For more than four (4) hours of work, the employer may provide and deduct no more than $1.10 each for up to two (2) meals furnished. Up to three-fourths of the rental value of lodging furnished may be deducted.

No more than $1.45 per hour may be deducted from the minimum wage, except that if an employee receives less than $1.45 per hour in tips, the credit can be no more than the tips actually received. The employer may not charge an employee or deduct for breakage, walkouts, mistakes on customer checks, or other similar charges. Other deductions are allowed only when required by Law or authorized by the worker for his/her own benefit.

CHILD LABOR LAW. No one under eighteen (18) may work (nor under 21 sell or serve) where alcoholic beverages are sold, except when a work permit is issued to a minor sixteen (16) to eighteen (18) who is the child of the proprietor, or one who operates an elevator.

All minors under eighteen (18) are limited to eight (8) hours per day, forty-eight (48) hours and six (6) days per week. Hours of employment are limited from 7 a.m. to 7 p.m. for females, and 6 a.m. to 10 p.m. for males. Females in hotels, restaurants, and mercantile establishments may work only 7 a.m. to 6 p.m. under current District of Columbia Law, but these provisions are of questionable validity in light of sex discrimination cases.

All minors under eighteen (18) employed in the entertainment field must get a work permit from the Board of Education.

No one under eighteen (18) may work with power-driven machinery.

Minors fourteen (14) to sixteen (16) must obtain a work permit, and females under sixteen (16) may work only 7 a.m. to 7 p.m.

No child under fourteen (14) may be employed except one over ten (10) years old as a newsboy/girl and one over seven (7) in a theatrical and musical entertainment job.

Please note all sex distinction regarding employment of minors has been ruled inoperable under Title VII of the Civil Rights Act of 1964, as amended.

UNIFORM MAINTENANCE. When the employer purchases, but the employee cleans (plain and washable) uniforms, the employer shall pay $.05 per hour over the minimum wage. When the employee purchases and cleans such uniforms, the employer shall pay $.07 per hour over the minimum wage. When the employee purchases, but the employer cleans such uniforms, the employer shall pay $.02 over the minimum wage. The employer is to pay for the purchase, maintenance, and cleaning of protective clothing and special costumes.

FLORIDA WAGE & HOUR LAW

LAW. There are no Florida Laws governing minimum wages.

MINIMUM WAGE. No provision.

OVERTIME. No provision, except that some extra pay must be provided for hours of manual labor worked over ten (10), unless a written contract requires more or less work per day.

CREDITS. No provision.

CHILD LABOR LAW. No one under eighteen (18) may work where alcoholic beverages are sold. However, a seventeen-year-old (17) high school senior may apply for permission to work in such employment.

Hours are limited from 5 a.m. to 11 p.m., or 5 a.m. to 1 a.m. if the next day is a non-school day. An age certificate is required.

No one under sixteen (16) may work with power driven machinery, except power mowers with blades forty (40) inches or less; on scaffolding; in the operation of any motor vehicle; with meat grinders; or with power-driven bakery equipment. No one under sixteen (16) may work over ten (10) hours per day and forty (40) hours per week.

Generally, minors under sixteen (16) may work no more than four (4) hours if the following day is a school day. Hours are limited from 6:30 a.m. to 9 p.m.

Minors over fourteen (14) may work until 11 p.m. if the next day is a non-school day. An employment certificate must be obtained from school officials.

GEORGIA WAGE & HOUR LAW

LAW. Georgia's Wage & Hour Law covers all employers, except those subject to the Federal Wage & Hour Law whose sales are less than $40,000.00 per year, and those with less than five employees. The Law does not apply to employees whose wages are wholly or partly made up of tips, and to those who are high school and college students.

MINIMUM WAGE. The minimum wage is $1.25 per hour.

OVERTIME. No provision, although the maximum legal work-week is a ten-hour (10) day and a sixty-hour (60) week.

CREDITS. No provision.

EQUAL PAY. Georgia's Equal Pay Act requires employers with ten or more employees to refrain from discriminating on the basis of sex. Employees of one sex must not be paid at a rate less than that paid to employees of the opposite sex for comparable work.

CHILD LABOR LAW. No one under eighteen (18) may dispense, serve, sell, or take orders for any alcoholic beverages, or work where alcoholic beverages are sold for consumption on the premises. Minors under eighteen (18) must obtain a work permit.

No one under sixteen (16) may work during school hours (unless he/she has completed high school); work more than four (4) hours on a school day; work more than eight (8) hours on a non-school day; and work more than forty (40) hours per week.

Minors under sixteen (16) may work from 6 a.m. to 9 p.m. They may not operate power-driven machinery, boats, or motor vehicles; work in a bowling alley, elevator, or "picture-show machine"; or work in any occupation dangerous to life, limb, health, or morals.

A minor age fifteen (15) may pursue any occupation, not specifically prohibited by Law, during school vacation months.

Minors under fourteen (14) may not be employed in any gainful occupation, except those twelve (12) to fourteen (14) may be employed in stores by parents, and children working outside school hours may be employed by parents in private homes and in agriculture.

HAWAII WAGE & HOUR LAW

LAW. Hawaii's Wage & Hour Law covers all employees, except supervisors with a guaranteed monthly salary greater than $700.00; those covered by the Federal Wage & Hour Law, unless the Hawaii rate is greater; professional employees; those individuals employed by a relative; golf caddies, etc.

MINIMUM WAGE. The Hawaii minimum wage is $2.65 an hour as of July 1, 1978; $2.90 in 1979; $3.10 in 1980; $3.35 in 1981. Students may be employed in seasonal employment at not less than eighty-five percent (85%) of the minimum wage. Lower wages may be paid to learners, part-time employees who are students, and handicapped and disabled employees with the approval of the Director of Labor.

OVERTIME. Overtime is required for all hours worked in excess of forty (40) hours in one workweek and must be paid at the rate of at least time and one-half the regular rate of pay of the employee.

CREDITS. Tipped employees (those receiving at least $20.00 a month in tips as a regular and customary part of their jobs) must be paid no less than $.20 below the minimum wage, so long as the combined amount, *i.e.*, the employer-paid wage and the tips, exceeds the minimum wage by $.50. Meals, lodging, etc., may be added to wages paid.

EQUAL PAY. Employers may not discriminate in paying wages on the basis of race, sex, or religion.

CHILD LABOR LAW. No one under eighteen (18) may sell or serve alcoholic beverages, except in an approved job-training program for waiters and waitresses. They may not be employed in the theatre without an employment certificate, or in any occupation hazardous to life, health, safety, or well-being. Employment certificates are required.

No one under sixteen (16) may work during school hours. Further, work hours are limited to eight (8) hours per day, forty (40) hours per week, and six (6) days per week. The combined hours of work and school may not exceed ten (10) hours in one day. No more than five (5) hours of continuous work may be performed without a thirty-minute (30) break. Minors may work only from 7 a.m. to 7 p.m., except they may be employed from 6 a.m. to 8 p.m. June 1 to Labor Day.

SPLIT-SHIFT PAY. Split shifts worked by employees must come within fourteen (14) consecutive hours when they occur within a period of twenty-four (24) hours, except in the case of an emergency.

IDAHO WAGE & HOUR LAW

LAW. Idaho's Wage & Hour Law covers all employees, except those working in executive, administrative, and professional capacities. Additionally, it is inapplicable to minors under sixteen (16) working odd hours, and to those working part-time no more than four (4) hours per week.

MINIMUM WAGE. The current minimum wage, effective July 1, 1977, is $2.30 an hour. Learners and apprentices may be paid less with the issuance of a special license. Further, a special license from the Director of Labor and Industrial Services will allow the employment of handicapped persons at a rate below the minimum wage for not more than one year.

OVERTIME. Overtime is required for all hours in excess of eight (8) hours per day and forty-eight (48) hours per week. The overtime rate is time and one-half the regular rate of pay.

CREDITS. Meals may be credited as wages up to $.50 per day. No tip credit is allowed.

CHILD LABOR LAW. No one under nineteen (19) may serve alcoholic beverages.

No one under eighteen (18) may work where alcoholic beverages are sold for consumption on the premises.

No one under sixteen (16) may be employed during school hours, unless he/she can read and write, and has a fundamental knowledge of geography and arithmetic. They may not work in any theatrical or hazardous employment. Working hours for children under sixteen (16) are limited to nine (9) hours per day, between the hours of 6 a.m. and 9 p.m., and fifty-four (54) hours per week.

An employer shall maintain a list of minors fourteen (14) to sixteen (16) employed in all hotels, restaurants, stores, etc.

No one under fourteen (14) may work during school hours, or in a hotel, restaurant, or store.

ILLINOIS WAGE & HOUR LAW

LAW. Illinois's Wage & Hour Law is applicable to all employers, except those with less than four full-time employees and immediate family members.

MINIMUM WAGE. Effective January 1, 1977, the Illinois minimum wage became $2.30 per hour. Minors under eighteen (18) may be paid $1.95 per hour, and learners may be paid $1.50 per hour for up to six (6) months. Handicapped workers may be paid a lower wage with permission from the Department of Labor.

OVERTIME. The maximum workweek is eight (8) hours per day and forty-eight (48) hours per week. Time and one-half the regular rate of pay is required for hours over forty (40) in one week. Restaurant employees are paid time and one-half for hours in excess of forty-six (46) per week.

CREDITS. A tip credit of up to fifty percent (50%) of the minimum wage may be taken. Other deductions are allowed only where required by Law or authorized by the employee.

CHILD LABOR LAW. No one under twenty-one (21) may be employed as a driver of a motor vehicle carrying passengers.

No one under eighteen (18) may sell, deliver, or dispense alcoholic beverages to be consumed on the premises or drive a motor vehicle used as a carrier of property.

No one under sixteen (16) may work in any place of amusement; as a bellboy/girl in a hotel; about power-driven machinery; in the operation of freight elevators; in any place where intoxicating beverages are sold on the premises; in any occupation involving exposure to radioactive substances; or in any theatrical production without a certificate of employment. The hours of work are limited to eight (8) hours per day, forty (40) hours and six (6) days per week. On school days, three (3) hours of work and a total of eight (8) hours per day, for both school and work, is allowed.

No more than five (5) hours may be worked continuously without a thirty-minute (30) break. Minors may be employed from 7 a.m. to 7 p.m., except from 7 a.m. to 9 p.m. June 1 to Labor Day.

In theatrical productions, minors are limited to six (6) hours per day, twenty-four (24) hours and six (6) days per week. Additionally, they may not work later than 11 p.m.

INDIANA WAGE & HOUR LAW

LAW. Indiana's Wage & Hour Law covers all employers with more than four employees at work during a workweek. The Law does not cover persons under eighteen (18), and those employed by a parent or spouse. It does not cover employees in executive and administrative occupations earning $100.00 or more per week, or persons not employed for more than twenty (20) weeks in any four consecutive three-month periods.

MINIMUM WAGE. Indiana minimum wage is $1.25 per hour.

OVERTIME. Eight hours (8) is the legal workday in Indiana, but employees and employers may agree that extra pay be given for work in excess of eight (8) hours per day.

CREDITS. Tips and meals may be credited toward the minimum wage, so long as they do not exceed fifty percent (50%) of the minimum rate.

Twenty-five cents is allowed for light meals and $.50 for full meals.

Clothing may be credited up to $.35 a day when the employer furnishes, maintains, and launders uniforms.

Tips may be credited up to $.50 per hour for employees serving food food and alcoholic beverages, and those in bell and door services. Thirty-five cents per hour may be credited for those serving food only. The lodging credit is set at $1.00 per day, $5.00 per week, and $20.00 per month.

EQUAL PAY. Equal pay for equivalent work, regardless of sex, is required.

CHILD LABOR LAW. No one under twenty-one (21) may work in establishments where alcoholic beverages are sold, provided that those over eighteen (18) may work in such establishments in capacities in which they are not required to sell, furnish, or deal in alcoholic beverages. No one under eighteen (18) may work where alcoholic beverages are sold, or in any poolroom or billiard hall.

No one under seventeen (17) may work around hazardous, power-driven equipment, operate an elevator, etc.

Hours are limited to eight (8) hours per day, forty (40) hours and six (6) days per week, only between 6 a.m. and 10 p.m., except to midnight during summer vacation and with parents' permission.

Employment certificates are required.

No one under sixteen (16) may work more than three (3) hours per day and twenty-three (23) hours per week during the school term; no more than nine (9) hours per day and forty-eight (48) hours per week during summer vacation.

Minors fourteen (14) to sixteen (16) may not work later than 7 p.m. on a day preceding a school day, or 9 p.m. if the next day is not a school day.

IOWA WAGE & HOUR LAW

LAW. There is no Wage & Hour Law in Iowa.

MINIMUM WAGE. No provision.

OVERTIME. No provision.

CREDITS. No provision.

CHILD LABOR LAW. No one under eighteen (18) may work in an establishment where alcoholic beverages are sold for consumption on the premises, unless fifty percent (50%) of the gross business is the sale of food, and the minor is not involved in selling or serving alcoholic beverages. Minors under eighteen (18) also are prohibited from operating certain types of hazardous power-driven equipment, operating elevators, or doing any work involving exposure to radiation.

No one under sixteen (16) may work during school hours, unless legally out of school. Hours are limited to eight (8) hours per day; forty (40) hours per week (7 a.m. to 7 p.m., except 7 a.m. to 7 p.m. from June 1 to Labor Day); and a thirty-minute (30) rest period after five (5) hours of work. When school is in session, hours are limited to four (4) hours per day and twenty-eight (28) hours per week.

No one under fifteen (15) may work in cooking, except at soda fountains, lunch counters, cafeterias, or baking. They may not work with power-driven food slicers, grinders, choppers, cutters, or bakery-type mixers; work in freezers or meat coolers; wash outside windows above ground level; operate any power-driven machinery; or work in boiler rooms.

KANSAS WAGE & HOUR LAW

LAW. Kansas's Wage & Hour Law applies only to females and minors, and is set by order of the Commission on Wages of the Department of Labor.

MINIMUM WAGE. There is no fixed minimum wage in Kansas.

OVERTIME. There is no specific provision, but the maximum workweek is eight (8) hours per day and forty-eight (48) hours per week.

CREDITS. No provision.

EQUAL PAY. An employer may not discriminate by paying employees of one sex more than employees of the other on the basis of their sex.

CHILD LABOR LAW. No one under eighteen (18) may dispense alcoholic beverages for a cereal malt-beverage licensee, in public dance halls, or in any occupation hazardous to life, health, safety, welfare, or morals.
No one under sixteen (16) may work in any hotel, restaurant, store, theatre, or elevator, except by permit.
Minors under fourteen (14) may not be employed, except by their parents.

KENTUCKY WAGE & HOUR LAW

LAW. Kentucky's Wage & Hour Law is applicable to all employees, except learners; students under special permits; and restaurants with a gross income of less than $95,000.00 per year for the five (5) preceding years, exclusive of excise taxes at retail. Children of employers operating restaurants are exempted, and supervisors are also exempted.

MINIMUM WAGE. The minimum wage is $2.00 per hour as of July 1, 1978; $2.15 in 1979. Students may be paid eighty-five percent (85%) of the minimum wage up to twenty (20) hours of work per week.

OVERTIME. Overtime is required for hours over forty (40), and all hours on the seventh consecutive day of the workweek at the rate of time and one-half the regular rate of pay. This over-time requirement, however, is inapplicable to retail store employees engaged in work related to selling, purchasing, and distributing merchandise wares, goods, and commodities; to restaurant employees; and to hotel and motel employees.

CREDITS. Tips may be credited toward the minimum wage if the employee customarily receives more than $20.00 a month in tips. Employers may take a maximum tip credit of fifty percent (50%) of the minimum wage, provided the employer does not pay less than $.75 per hour. Meals may also be credited toward the minimum wage according to their reasonable value.

CHILD LABOR LAW. No one under twenty-one (21) may operate for hire a motor vehicle carrying passengers. No one under twenty (20) may work in any establishment licensed under the Alcoholic Beverage Laws.

No one under eighteen (18) may operate for hire a motor vehicle carrying property, or work in any occupation without an employment certificate from the Board of Education. Minors under eighteen (18) may not work more than eight (8) hours per day and forty-eight (48) hours per week when school is not in session, and four (4) hours per day and thirty-two (32) hours per week when school is in session. Hours are limited from 6 a.m. to 10 p.m. Sunday through Thursday, and 6 a.m. to midnight on Friday, except 6 a.m. to midnight on all days during school vacations.

Minors sixteen (16) to eighteen (18) who have graduated from high school may work ten (10) hours per day and sixty (60) hours per week. No one under eighteen (18) may be required to work over five (5) hours continuously without a thirty-minute (30) lunch break.

Minors fourteen (14) to sixteen (16) may not work outside washing windows above ground level; cooking (except soda fountains, lunch counters, snack bars, and cafeteria serving lines) or baking; with power-driven food slicers, grinders, choppers, cutters or bakery mixers; in freezers, meat coolers, warehouses, or boiler rooms; or operate a motor vehicle for hire. Hours are limited to eight (8) per day and forty (40) per week when school is not in session, and three (3) per day and eighteen (18) per week when school is in session. Limited hours are 7 a.m. to 7 p.m., except 7 a.m. to 9 p.m. between June 1 and Labor Day.

Minors under fourteen (14) generally may not be employed, except as golf caddies, and in and around the home or farm.

LOUISIANA WAGE & HOUR LAW

LAW. There is no Wage & Hour Law in Louisiana.

MINIMUM WAGE. No provision.

OVERTIME. No provision.

CREDITS. No provision.

CHILD LABOR LAW. No one under eighteen (18) may work where alcoholic beverages are sold for consumption on the premises, or operate an elevator.

No one under seventeen (17) may work over forty-four (44) hours per week and may work only from 6 a.m. to 10 p.m.

No one under sixteen (16) may work with power-driven machinery, in a poolroom, or in theatrical employment without a special permit from the Commissioner of Labor.

Minors under sixteen (16) may work only outside school hours. They may work no more than three (3) hours per day, and from 6 a.m. to 7 p.m. when school is in session. Theatrical performers may work from 6 a.m. to 11 p.m.

No one under fourteen (14) may pursue any occupation other than golf caddy, newsboy/girl, and other "street trades".

MAINE WAGE & HOUR LAW

LAW. Maine's Wage & Hour Law covers all employers and employees, except those in the family of the employer, tipped employees who receive more than $20.00 a month in tips, and those in supervisory and professional capacities earning more than $150.00 per week.

MINIMUM WAGE. The minimum wage is $2.65 per hour. The Maine minimum wage is to be increased along with the Federal minimum wage, but not to exceed $3.00 per hour. Student employees under nineteen (19) years of age must be paid not less than seventy-five percent (75%) of the applicable minimum wage.

OVERTIME. Hotels, motels, and restaurants are exempt from the overtime provision of Maine's Wage & Hour Law. The overtime provision, where applicable, requires overtime after forty (40) hours at time and one-half the regular rate of pay.

CREDITS. A tip credit may be taken up to fifty percent (50%) of the minimum wage. Room and board may be deducted according to a schedule published by the Bureau of Labor and Industry.

EQUAL PAY. Equal pay for comparable work, classification, and experience is required, regardless of sex.

CHILD LABOR LAW. No one under eighteen (18) may serve alcoholic beverages to be consumed on the premises, except in a Class "A" restaurant where a seventeen-year-old (17) may serve alcoholic beverages under the supervision of an employee who is over eighteen (18). Additionally, no one under eighteen (18) may operate power-driven food slicers, choppers, grinders, mixers, or bakery equipment.

No one under sixteen (16) may operate an elevator in a hotel, or any elevator traveling over 200 feet per minute. The hours are limited to four (4) hours per day, twenty-eight (28) hours and six (6) days per week when school is in session, and eight (8) hours per day, forty-eight (48) hours and six (6) days per week when school is not in session.

Minors under sixteen (16) may work only from 7 a.m. to 9 p.m., and employment certificates are required.

No one under fifteen (15) may operate any elevator.

MARYLAND WAGE & HOUR LAW

LAW. Employers who employ one or more employees are covered by Maryland's Wage & Hour Law. However, the Law does not apply to employees or employers covered by the Federal Wage & Hour Law, or to employees employed by restaurants, taverns, cafes, and theatres with gross receipts of less than $250,000.00 a year which serve food or drink for consumption on the premises. The Law does not cover employees employed by a family member; minors under the age of sixteen (16) who work less than twenty (20) hours per week; and persons sixty-two (62) and over who work twenty-five (25) hours or less per week.

MINIMUM WAGE. The Maryland minimum wage is the same as the Federal minimum wage, which is $2.30 per hour.

OVERTIME. The overtime provisions of the Maryland Wage & Hour Law do not apply to hotels, motels, restaurants, country clubs, seasonal amusement and recreational establishments. Where applicable, overtime is required for all hours over forty (40) per week at time and one-half the regular rate of pay.

CREDITS. A tip credit may be taken for tipped employees making over $20.00 a month in tips up to fifty percent (50%) of the minimum wage. Meals may be credited by using the fair value of the meals against the minimum wage of the employee. The Commissioner of Labor determines the fair value of meals and lodging provided to employees.

EQUAL PAY. Equal pay for comparable work, regardless of sex, is required.

CHILD LABOR LAW. No one under twenty-one (21) may call for, or deliver a telegram or message at a house of ill repute.

No one under twenty-one (21) may be employed in the sale of alcoholic beverages on the premises of a Class "D" licensee. In Carroll County, eighteen (18) years old is the limit generally for the sale of beer and light wine, and in Prince George's County, eighteen (18) is the limit for the sale of all alcoholic beverages.

No one under eighteen (18) may work in gainful employment without an employment certificate, or in any occupation hazardous to life, health, or welfare. Child Labor hours are limited from 6 a.m. to 11 p.m. for those attending school.

No one under seventeen (17) may work more than five (5) hours per day, thirty (30) hours and six (6) days per week when school is in session, or eight (8) hours per day and forty (40) hours per week when school is not in session.

Minors sixteen (16) and eighteen (18), who are attending school, may work only between 6 a.m. and 11 p.m. Those not attending school may work nine (9) hours per day and forty-eight (48) hours per week.

No one under sixteen (16) may work in a hotel, restaurant, theatre, or elevator; with hazardous, power-driven machinery; or during school hours. Work is limited to six (6) days per week, three (3) hours per day, and twenty-three (23) hours per week when school is in session, and eight (8) hours per day and forty (40) hours per week when school is not in session. Hours are limited from 7 a.m. to 7 p.m., except from 7 a.m. to 9 p.m. June 1 to Labor Day.

MASSACHUSETTS WAGE & HOUR LAW

LAW. Massachusetts's Wage & Hour Law covers all persons in all jobs and occupations. However, the Massachusetts Commissioner of Labor and Industries may authorize the payment of subminimum wages to learners, apprentices, and handicapped persons. The payment of subminimum wages is allowed only when approval has been granted by the Commissioner. Wages and working conditions are set by Statute and by order of the Commissioner. Order No. 25-D deals with hotels, motels, and restaurants.

MINIMUM WAGE. The minimum wage is $2.65 per hour, except for learners, apprentices, and handicapped workers. Also, tipped employees who receive more than $20.00 a month in tips must be paid only $1.20 per hour or sixty percent (60%) of the minimum wage.

OVERTIME. The overtime provisions of the Massachusetts Wage & Hour Law do not apply to hotel, motel, and restaurant employees or to learners, apprentices, and handicapped persons. However, an employer may not require employees to work more than six (6) consecutive days. Where the over-time provisions are applicable, time and one-half the regular rate of pay is required for hours in excess of forty (40) per workweek.

CREDITS. Tipped employees must be paid at least sixty percent (60%) of the minimum wage.

Meal credits may be taken up to $.50 per meal if the employee gives his/her written consent. Such meals must be actually furnished, well-balanced nutritionally, and the servings must be of ample size.

Uniforms must be furnished and maintained by the employer.

Lodging may be deducted at the rate of $4.00 per week if not more than two (2) employees occupy a room, and at $3.25 per week if more than two (2) employees occupy a room.

CHILD LABOR LAW. No one under eighteen (18) may work where alcoholic beverages are sold, operate an elevator, operate a motion-picture projector, work as a security guard, or work more than thirty (30) feet above ground level. Hours are limited from 6 a.m. to 10 p.m., except in restaurants until midnight preceding a non-schoolday.

No one under sixteen (16) may work on scaffolding; in an elevator, bowling alley, or poolroom; or during school hours. Hours are limited to eight (8) hours per day, forty-eight (48) hours and six (6) days a week, between 6:30 a.m. and 6 p.m., or until sundown as a golf caddie.

Minors under fourteen (14) generally may not be gainfully employed.

REPORT IN PAY. Employees required to report for work at the request of the employer or at regularly scheduled times, must be paid at least four (4) hours pay.

MEAL PERIODS. Massachusetts Law requires that all employees receive one thirty-minute (30) meal period during a six-hour (6) work period. The meal period does not have to be a paid period.

MICHIGAN WAGE & HOUR LAW

LAW. Michigan's Wage & Hour Law applies to all employers with four or more employees at any one time within the calendar year. Persons under eighteen (18) and over sixty-four (64) years of age are exempt from coverage. Employers covered by the Federal Wage & Hour Law are not covered, unless a lower wage would be paid under the Federal Law.

MINIMUM WAGE. The minimum wage is $2.65 an hour. Effective January 1, 1979, it is $2.90; January 1, 1980–$3.10; January 1, 1981–$3.25.

OVERTIME. Employees of hotels, motels, restaurants, and certain mercantile establishments are not covered by the overtime pay provisions of the Michigan Wage & Hour Law, unless such employees are exempt from the Federal Wage & Hour Law overtime requirement. Where applicable, overtime is required for all hours over forty (40) at the rate of time and one-half the regular rate of pay.

CREDITS. A tip credit is allowed up to twenty-five percent (25%) of the Michigan minimum wage. Tips may be credited only to the extent that they are declared for the Federal Insurance Contribution Act and the employee is notified of the tip credit provision.

Meals and uniform apparel may be credited up to twenty-five percent (25%) of the minimum wage. Meals may be credited at $.03 an hour per light meal and $.05 an hour per regular meal.

Lodging may be credited toward the minimum wage up to $.08 per hour for single occupancy and $.04 per hour for multiple occupancy. Other facilities connected with lodging may be credited toward the minimum wage according to a schedule issued by the Wage Deviation Board.

CHILD LABOR LAW. No one under eighteen (18) may work where alcoholic beverages are sold for consumption on the premises, except where food constitutes fifty percent (50%) of gross receipts. They may not work in hazardous occupations, unless they are over seventeen (17) and high school graduates. They may not work as motion-picture projectionists, operate elevators, or work where there is exposure to ionizing radiation. Their hours are limited to ten (10) hours per day, forty-eight (48) hours and six (6) days per week (or a combined school and workweek of forty-eight (48) hours). There must be a thirty-minute (30) break after five (5) hours of work. The maximum time period for minors attending school is 6 a.m. to 10:30 p.m., and 11:30 p.m. is the maximum time limit otherwise. Employment certificates are required.

No one under seventeen (17) may be required to lift over fifty (50) pounds in the course of employment.

No one under sixteen (16) may work away from home without the consent of a parent or truant officer; or in any theatre, dance hall, or billiard room, except in a theatrical company with a permit from the Department of Labor and Industry. Hours are limited from 7 a.m. to 9 p.m., except in theatrical performances which run later.

No one under fifteen (15) may work during school hours in any store, office, hotel, theatre, billiard room, elevator, or bowling alley.

No one under fourteen (14) may be employed, except as a golf caddie.

MINNESOTA WAGE & HOUR LAW

LAW. Minnesota's Wage & Hour Law covers all nonsupervisory employees and is implemented by the Commissioner of Labor and Industry.

MINIMUM WAGE. The minimum wage is $2.10 per hour, and $1.89 for minors under eighteen (18). For learners and apprentices, the rate is $1.62 for the first 300 hours of employment. Lower rates may be set for handicapped employees by permit from the Labor Standards Division.

OVERTIME. Overtime is required at the rate of time and one-half the regular rate of pay for all hours over forty-eight (48) in a work-week. Employers covered only by the Minnesota Wage & Hour Law may give time off at the rate of one and one-half hours for any hour over forty-eight (48) instead of monetary compensation for overtime hours.

CREDITS. A tip credit may be taken for tipped employees who regularly receive $35.00 a month or more in tips up to twenty percent (20%) of the minimum wage, if the employee signs a statement indicating that he/she receives tips in an amount equal to or greater than twenty percent (20%) of the minimum wage.

A meal credit of $.90 per meal is allowed if accepted by the employee. An employer may not require employees to accept meals as a condition of employment. Further, it is illegal to deduct from an employee's minimum wage for breakage and for maintenance and/or purchase of uniforms. No credit is allowed for uniform maintenance or purchase.

No deductions are allowed for shortages in cash receipts.

A lodging credit of $1.15 per day may be taken if accepted by the employee.

EQUAL PAY. Equal pay for equal work is required under the Minnesota Wage & Hour Law.

CHILD LABOR LAW. No one under eighteen (18) may work where alcoholic beverages are sold for consumption on the premises, except as musicians, busboys/girls, and dishwashers in restaurants, hotels, and motels where food is served in the same rooms with alcoholic beverages.

No one under sixteen (16) may work on school days without an employment certificate. Hours are limited to eight (8) per day, forty (40) per week, between 7 a.m. and 9:30 p.m.

No one under fourteen (14) may work, except as an actor, model, performer, and newspaper carrier.

MEAL PERIODS. Meal, break, and rest periods of less than twenty (20) minutes may not be deducted from an employee's hours worked.

PAYMENT OF WAGES. Wages must be paid at least biweekly. Wages due strikers must be paid at the next regular payday.

MISSISSIPPI WAGE & HOUR LAW

LAW. There is no Wage & Hour Law in Mississippi.

MINIMUM WAGE. No provision.

OVERTIME. No provision.

CREDITS. No provision.

CHILD LABOR LAW. Alcoholic Beverage Commission Regulation 17 prohibits employing anyone under twenty-one (21) in the sale of alcoholic beverages, except where it is for the purpose of handling and selling food only, or as an entertainer.

MISSOURI WAGE & HOUR LAW

LAW. There is no Wage & Hour Law in Missouri, except the Equal Pay for Equal Work Provision.

MINIMUM WAGE. No provision.

OVERTIME. No provision.

CREDITS. No provision.

EQUAL PAY. Equal pay for equal work is required.

CHILD LABOR LAW. No one under twenty-one (21) may be employed in selling intoxicating liquors.
No one under sixteen (16) may work in any place where intoxicating liquors are sold for consumption; in any saloon, hotel, or motel; on scaffolding; in the operation of a motor vehicle or freight elevator; or in any other occupation hazardous to life, health, limb, or morals.
Hours of minors under sixteen (16) are limited to eight (8) per day, forty (40) per week, and six (6) days per week. If the next day is a school

day, they may work only from 7 a.m. to 7 p.m.; if the next day is not a school day, they may work only from 7 a.m. to 10 p.m. (unless permanently excused from school). Work certificates are required.

MONTANA WAGE & HOUR LAW

LAW. Montana's Wage & Hour Law is applicable to all employees, except learners; those in the employer's immediate family; those who receive fifty percent (50%) support from the employer's family; retired or semiretired employees; part-time employees; and supervisory personnel. Learners are exempt only during their first thirty (30) days of employment.

MINIMUM WAGE. The minimum wage is $2.00 an hour.

OVERTIME. Generally, overtime is required at time and one-half the regular rate of pay for all hours over forty (40) in a workweek. For students employed at a recreational area operating seasonally, time and one-half the regular rate of pay is required for all hours over forty-eight (48) in a workweek, if they are furnished with meals and lodging.

CREDITS. A tip credit may be taken by the employer. The reasonable value of meals and lodging up to forty percent (40%) of the minimum wage may be credited.

EQUAL PAY. Equal pay for equivalent work, regardless of sex, is required.

CHILD LABOR LAW. No one under eighteen (18) may work as a bartender or waiter/waitress whose duty it is to serve intoxicating liquors.
No one under sixteen (16) may work in an elevator, or in any operation hazardous to health or morals.

PAYMENT OF WAGES. Employers must pay wages earned within ten (10) days of the date when they become due and payable.

MISCELLANEOUS. Employees in commercial eating establishments must have twelve (12) hours off duty following eight (8) hours of work.
Employers operating restaurants, cafes, bars, and other eating establishments are required to place mats of non-slippery materials in front of all stoves, sinks, and other articles of equipment where employees customarily stand.

NEBRASKA WAGE & HOUR LAW

LAW. Nebraska's Wage & Hour Law applies to employers with four or more employees at any one time, exclusive of seasonal employees hired for less than twenty (20) weeks. Learners, supervisors, and children working for a parent are not covered.

MINIMUM WAGE. The minimum wage is $1.60 per hour. Tipped employees such as waiters/waitresses, bell service employees, and the like may be paid the rate of $.90 per hour plus tips. The employer must approve the tips received by the employee.

OVERTIME. No provision.

CREDITS. Tipped employees must be paid at least $.90 per hour.

EQUAL PAY. Equal pay for equivalent work is required.

CHILD LABOR LAW. No one under eighteen (18) may dispense alcoholic beverages in any tavern or public place.

No one under sixteen (16) may work without an employment certificate in a hotel, motel, restaurant, elevator, store, office, theatre, or place of amusement. Hours are limited to those between 6 a.m. and 10 p.m.

No one under fourteen (14) may work in any business during school hours, or in the above-listed occupations at any time.

However, children fourteen (14) to sixteen (16) may work as golf caddies. Their hours are limited to those between 6 a.m. and 8 p.m.

NEVADA WAGE & HOUR LAW

LAW. Applicable to all employees.

MINIMUM WAGE. The minimum wage is the same as the Federal rate.

OVERTIME. Overtime is time and one-half for hours over eight (8) in a workday and forty (40) in a workweek, unless set by agreement at hours over ten (10) in a day. This does not apply to businesses with gross sales of less than $250,000.00 in 1977. Overtime is not required for employees receiving regular hourly compensation at one and one-half times the minimum rate, and for supervisory and managerial personnel.

CREDITS. Tip credits are not allowed in Nevada.

The employer and employee may agree to credit meals as part of wages up to $1.50 per day, or $.35 for breakfast, $.45 for lunch, and $.70 for dinner.

No uniform costs may be deducted. Employers must pay for special cleaning such as dry cleaning.

CHILD LABOR LAW. No one under eighteen (18) may be employed in any dance hall where women are employed. A minor is prohibited from selling alcoholic beverages for consumption on the premises.

A minor over sixteen (16) may sell sealed containers of alcoholic beverages for consumption off the premises if he/she is supervised.

No one under sixteen (16) may work more than eight (8) hours per day and forty (40) hours per week.

No one under fourteen (14) may be employed away from the house or farm.

MEALS. One meal period of thirty (30) minutes is required every eight (8) hours, and a ten-minute (10) paid rest period is required every four (4) hours.

NEW HAMPSHIRE WAGE & HOUR LAW

LAW. New Hampshire's Wage & Hour Law covers all employees, except those covered by the Federal Wage & Hour Law, and those employed by a parent, grandparent, guardian, or spouse. The Law is also inapplicable to golf caddies.

MINIMUM WAGE. The minimum wage is related to the Federal minimum wage and is presently $2.30 per hour. Employees under eighteen (18), or with less than six (6) months' experience, may be paid seventy-five percent (75%) of the applicable minimum wage under State Wage & Hour Law, after an application is filed with the Labor Commissioner, and within ten (10) days of hiring.

OVERTIME. No provision.

CREDITS. Employees of restaurants, hotels, motels, and the like may have their wages calculated by including meals provided at no more than $.80 per day and $16.80 per week; full room and board at $3.60 per day and $24.00 per week; and lodging only at $1.20 per day and $7.25 per week.

A tip credit of up to fifty percent (50%) of the minimum wage may be taken.

No credit may be taken for uniforms.

No deductions may be taken, except where required by Law, or requested by the employee for his/her own benefit.

EQUAL PAY. New Hampshire has an Equal Pay Law, which requires equal pay for equivalent work, regardless of sex.

CHILD LABOR LAW. No one under eighteen (18) may handle alcoholic beverages sold for consumption on the premises, or obtain a chauffeur's license.

Minors sixteen (16) to eighteen (18) who cannot read and speak English may not be employed in a district that has an evening or special day school without a certificate showing enrollment in, or permitting absence from, such school.

No one under sixteen (16) may be employed when schools are in session, except a minor who can read and write simple English sentences; golf caddies; and those who work for religious organizations. Hours are limited from 7 a.m. to 9 p.m., three (3) hours per day and twenty-three (23) hours per week when schools are in session. They are limited to eight (8) hours per day and forty-eight (48) hours per week during vacations.

No one under fourteen (14) may work in any occupation away from home or farm, except as golf caddie, newsboy/girl, or in a religious organization.

No one under twelve (12) may work in any occupation, except for a parent, grandparent, or guardian, and in newspaper delivery.

PAYMENT OF WAGES AND REPORT IN PAY. Wages must be paid weekly under New Hampshire Wage & Hour Law, unless other arrangements are approved by the Labor Commissioner. Furthermore, employees must receive at least three (3) hours of pay on any day if reporting to work. Employees must receive their regular rates of pay for waiting time. Additionally, employers must maintain a medical chest with supplies for first aid at the expense of the employer.

NEW JERSEY WAGE & HOUR LAW

LAW. New Jersey's Wage & Hour Law applies to all employees. Wage Order No. 3 covers hotels and motels, and Wage Order No. 9 covers restaurants.

MINIMUM WAGE. The basic minimum wage in New Jersey is $2.50 per hour. This rate is inapplicable to employees under eighteen (18) years of age who do not possess a special vocational-school-graduate permit. Additionally, subminimum wage rates are appropriate when approved by the Commissioner for learners, apprentices, students, and handicapped workers.

OVERTIME. Time and one-half is required for all hours worked over forty (40) within the workweek.

CREDITS. Tips and the fair value of food and lodging actually accepted by employees may be deducted from the minimum hourly rate, except where there is a Collective Bargaining Agreement to the contrary. For hotel and motel food-service workers, and others for whom tips are customary, wages may not be less than fifty-eight percent (58%) of the minimum wage after allowances for tips, food, and lodging.

For hotel and motel chambermaids, wages may not be less than eighty-nine percent (89%) of the minimum wage after deduction of tips, and less than eighty-four percent (84%) after allowances for tips, food, and lodging.

In seasonal hotels and motels, however, wages may not fall below eighty percent (80%) of the minimum wage after allowance for gratuities, and not less than seventy-five percent (75%) after allowances for gratuities, food, and lodging. Other deductions are allowed only where required by Law or by the request of the employee.

EQUAL PAY. New Jersey has an Equal Pay Act, which requires equal pay for equivalent work, regardless of sex.

CHILD LABOR LAW. No one under eighteen (18) may sell or serve alcoholic beverages for consumption on the premises. However, minors sixteen (16) to eighteen (18) may work in a restaurant where alcoholic beverages are served, provided they do not engage in the sale and serving of alcoholic beverages, the sale of cigarettes and other tobacco products, the preparation and sale of photographs, or any dancing and theatrical exhibition. Hours are limited to eight (8) per day, forty (40) per week, and six (6) days per week; 6 a.m. to 10 p.m. during school session; 6 a.m. to 11 p.m. during school vacations; and 6 a.m. to 12 midnight (ages 16–18) in restaurants, if the next day is not a school day. Employment certificates are required. After five (5) continuous hours of work, employees must have a thirty-minute (30) meal break.

No one under sixteen (16) may be employed during school hours, or work with power-driven machinery. Hours for such employees are limited to eight (8) per day for both work and school, between 6 a.m. and 7 p.m.

Children over fourteen (14) may work as golf caddies and pool attendants.

NEW MEXICO WAGE & HOUR LAW

LAW. New Mexico's Wage & Hour Law applies to all employees, except apprentices, learners, supervisors, and students (other than college students), working after school hours and during vacations.

MINIMUM WAGE. The minimum wage is $2.30 per hour. If an employee receives monthly tips of more than $40.00, the minimum hourly wage is $1.50.

OVERTIME. The overtime provisions are applicable to restaurants, hotels, and other foodservice facilities. Hours worked are limited to ten (10) hours per day and seven (7) days per week. Since the Federal Rule is probably applicable, due to an unenforceable and sexually discriminatory State Overtime Law, time and one-half is required for all hours over forty-six (46). Furthermore, all employers engaged in interstate commerce are excluded from New Mexico's Wage & Hour Law overtime provisions.

CREDITS. New Mexico Criminal Law prohibits employers from compelling employees to purchase goods, foods, and services from the employer.

CHILD LABOR LAW. No one under twenty-one (21) may be employed to sell or serve alcoholic beverages. For all other purposes, the age of majority is eighteen (18).

No one under sixteen (16) may work with hazardous, power-driven equipment; operate nonautomatic elevators; or work in any employment dangerous to life, limb, health, or morals. These employees may not work during school hours without employment certificates; economic necessity must be shown before employment certificates will be issued.

No one under fourteen (14) may be employed in any gainful occupation outside the hours of 7 a.m. to 9 p.m.

NEW YORK WAGE & HOUR LAW

LAW. New York has elaborate Wage & Hour Laws covering all non-supervisory employees.

MINIMUM WAGE. The minimum wage is $2.30 per hour. The rate is $2.35 for part-time employees who work thirty (30) hours or less per week.

Minors under eighteen (18) may be paid $.35 per hour, provided there are no more than two (2) employees on any day, or ten percent (10%) of the total employees, whichever is greater, and they may be paid at minors' rates. Additionally, special rates may be set by the Commissioner for learners, apprentices, handicapped workers, student summer help, and other employees in resort hotels.

OVERTIME. Time and one-half is required for all hours over forty (40) in the workweek, except for residential employees in hotels who receive time and one-half for all hours over forty-four (44). In resort hotels, time and one-half is required for all hours worked on the seventh consecutive day.

CREDITS. *Restaurants:* A tip credit may be taken up to $.50

per hour for employees whose weekly average of tips received is $.50 to $.70 per hour. Up to $.70 per hour may be credited for employees whose weekly average of tips is $.70 per hour or higher. No tip credit may be taken for those who average less than $.50 per hour in tips.

A meal allowance may be taken for one meal per shift, or up to two (2) for shifts over five (5) hours.

No allowance for uniform supply or laundering may be taken; where employees must purchase uniforms, the employees must be reimbursed no later than the next payment of wages. Where the employer does not provide for laundering or maintenance of uniforms, he must pay an additional $2.90 per week to employees who work over thirty (30) hours, $2.20 per week to employees who work twenty (20) to thirty (30) hours, and $1.40 per week to employees who work twenty (20) hours or less.

All-Year Hotels: The tip credit provisions are the same as those for restaurants.

A meal allowance of up to $.80 per meal for meals received by employees during reasonable periods, and customarily eaten by employees, may be taken. Only one (1) meal credit may be taken for an employee working less than five (5) hours per day.

A lodging allowance of up to $.15 per hour may be taken.

Resort Hotels: A tip credit of up to $.75 per hour may be taken for employees whose weekly average of tips exceeds $1.50 per hour. For chambermaids, the tip credit is up to $.35 per hour if weekly tip average is $.35 to $1.50 per hour, and up to $.55 per hour if the weekly tip average exceeds $1.50 per hour.

Meals and lodging allowances up to $4.55 may be taken for each day worked. For meals without lodging, $.80 per meal is allowed. For lodging without meals, $.15 per hour is allowed.

CHILD LABOR LAWS. No one under eighteen (18) may sell, handle, or dispense alcoholic beverages for consumption on the premises; operate a nonautomatic elevator; work around ionizing radiation; operate hazardous, power-driven equipment; etc. Hours are limited to six (6) per day and forty-eight (48) per week, except for singers and performers at a seasonal or resort hotel or restaurant. These minors may work only between the hours of 6 a.m. and midnight. They may not work when school attendance is required by Law.

Minors sixteen (16) years old are limited to employment for three (3) hours on school days, eight (8) hours on non-school days, twenty-eight (28) hours and six (6) days per week. They may work only between 7 a.m. and 7 p.m. when school is not in session.

Minors under sixteen (16) are limited to employment for three (3) hours per day, twenty-three (23) hours and six (6) days per week during school session. When school is not in session, they are limited to eight (8) hours per day, six (6) days and forty (40) hours per week, between 7 a.m. and 7 p.m.

SPLIT SHIFT. New York's Wage & Hour Law defines a split

shift as daily working hours that are not consecutive, with hours or shifts that are split between the beginning and end of the employee's workday. An employee is entitled to a meal period of one (1) hour or less which is considered an interruption of consecutive hours. Restaurant workers must work two (2) or more periods within fourteen (14) consecutive hours.

WORK LIMITATION. New York's Wage & Hour Law has a work limitation of ten (10) hours per day, fifty-six (56) hours per week, and twelve (12) days in any period of fourteen (14) consecutive days.

NORTH CAROLINA WAGE & HOUR LAW

LAW. North Carolina's Wage & Hour Law applies to all employees, except those under twenty-one (21) employed by a parent, those under sixteen (16) who work for an employer with less than four employees (except for family), college students working part-time during school terms, and golf caddies.

MINIMUM WAGE. The minimum wage is $2.00 per hour, which does not fully apply to part-time employees working sixteen (16) or fewer hours per week if there are three or fewer full-time employees employed at the same job. Full-time students over sixteen (16) may receive not less than $1.40 per hour.

OVERTIME. Time and one-half is required for all hours over fifty (50) in a workweek. The overtime provisions are limited to employees over eighteen (18). Furthermore, the overtime provision does not apply to seasonal hotels and clubs. Employers with no more than three employees at each business establishment are also excluded from the overtime provisions.

CREDITS. Tips may be credited up to fifty percent (50%) of the minimum wage.
Meals may be credited at the rate of $.75 per meal, $2.25 per day, and $15.00 per week.
A lodging credit may be taken at the rate of $1.50 per day and $10.00 per week.
Full room and board may be deducted at the rate of $25.00 per week.
Other deductions may be made only where required by Law, or authorized by the employee for his/her benefit.

CHILD LABOR LAW. No one under eighteen (18) may work in any establishment where liquor is sold for consumption on the premises, except that a minor over sixteen (16) may work in a Class "A" restaurant where alcoholic beverages are sold, if the minor does not serve or dispense alcoholic beverages. Hours are limited to six (6) per day, forty (40) hours per week, from 6 a.m. to 12 midnight. An employment certificate is required.

No one under sixteen (16) may work during school hours, with power-driven machinery, or elevators. Hours are limited to those between 7 a.m. and 7 p.m. when school is in session, and 7 a.m. to 9 p.m. when school is not in session.

No one under fourteen (14) may be employed, except in farm or domestic work for the minor's parent or guardian.

NORTH DAKOTA WAGE & HOUR LAW

LAW. North Dakota's Wage & Hour Law covers all employees, including minors. It is implemented under Wage Order No. 1 for public housekeeping employees.

MINIMUM WAGE. The minimum wage is $2.20 per hour for waiters/waitresses, bartenders, busboys/girls, cooks, kitchen workers, and other foodservice workers. Learners, part-time or full-time, receive $1.60 per hour. Furthermore, the learning period may not exceed 150 hours. Part-time rates are the same as full-time rates.

OVERTIME. Overtime is required at time and one-half the regular rate for all hours over forty (40) within the workweek.

CREDITS. Neither tip credits nor meal credits may be taken in discharging an employer's responsibility to pay the minimum wage. Furthermore, pooling of tips cannot be compelled by an employer or other workers.

EQUAL PAY. Equal pay for equivalent work is required, regardless of sex.

MINORS. No one under twenty-one (21) may serve or dispense alcoholic beverages for consumption on the premises. However, minors under twenty-one (21) may be employed as foodwaiters/waitresses, busboys/girls, etc., in restaurants where alcoholic beverages are served, as long as they work under the supervision of someone over twenty-one (21) and do not deal with alcoholic beverages.

Minors eighteen (18) to twenty-one (21) may be employed as musicians in establishments where alcoholic beverages are sold, provided they are under the direct supervision of someone over twenty-one (21).

No one under eighteen (18) may be hired in a place where billiards, bowling, and cards are played; this also applies to persons over eighteen (18) who are still in high school. Their hours are limited to eight (8) per day, forty (40) hours and six (6) days per week.

No one under sixteen (16) may work with hazardous, power-driven machinery. Their hours are limited to eight (8) per day and forty-eight (48) per week when school is not in session; three (3) per day and twenty-four (24) per week when school is in session, unless exempted; and 7 a.m. to 7 p.m., except 7 a.m. to 9 p.m. between June 1 and Labor Day.

No one under fourteen (14) may be employed in any hotel, restaurant, store, or any business during school hours.

MEAL PERIOD. A thirty-minute (30) meal period which does not have to be paid must be granted during each eight-hour (8) work period.

SEPARATE WASHROOM FACILITIES. Separate washroom facilities must be provided for male and female employees.

OHIO WAGE & HOUR LAW

LAW. Ohio's Wage & Hour Law applies to all employers grossing over $95,000.00 annually.

MINIMUM WAGE. The minimum wage rate became $2.00 per hour on January 1, 1977. On July 1, 1977, it became $2.10 per hour; and effective December 31, 1977, the minimum wage in Ohio is $2.30 per hour.

For up to ninety (90) days, learners may be paid subminimum wages at the rate of eighty percent (80%) of the minimum wage, and apprentices may be paid eighty-five (85%) of the minimum wage. Subminimum rates are also set for handicapped workers.

The overtime rate under Ohio's Wage & Hour Law is consistent with the Federal Wage & Hour Law.

CREDITS. A tip credit of up to fifty percent (50%) of the minimum wage may be taken in the same manner as under Federal Law.

No deductions for breakage may be taken, except pursuant to an express contract.

No meal credit is allowed if the employee is required to take his meals at the employer's place of business, or if the compensation includes or is based on the employer's furnishing the meals. An employee charged for meals may agree to the employer's price as long as the price does not exceed $.30 for breakfast, $.45 for lunch, and $.65 for dinner. The employer and employee may agree to deduct up to $4.00 per week for lodging furnished. Unless there is an agreement, however, no lodging credit may be deducted. Uniform and equipment charges may not be credited.

There are various other Wage Orders and Provisions of the Ohio Wage & Hour Law which treat women and minors differently from men. Some of these provisions are no doubt unenforceable pursuant to sex discrimination cases and decisions.

CHILD LABOR LAW. No one under twenty-one (21) may deal with alcoholic beverages to be consumed on the premises, except that minors eighteen (18) to twenty-one (21) may work as busboys/girls, as dishwashers of empty containers or may handle sealed containers.

No one under eighteen (18) may work during school hours without a special certificate, or work where alcoholic beverages are sold for consumption on the premises, except when enrolled in a vocational training program. Such individuals may not work in a theatre or amusement place without a special certificate. Their hours are limited to eight (8) hours per day, forty-eight (48) hours and six (6) days per week; and 6 a.m. to 10 p.m., except to midnight if the following day is not a school day.

No one under sixteen (16) may work in a restaurant, hotel, or store or in any occupation, unless out of school due to graduation or exclusion because of mental deficiency.

SPLIT SHIFT. A split shift is defined as a working day which is divided into two or more periods, with such periods falling within ten consecutive hours. In the case of hotels or hospitals, the period must fall within twelve consecutive hours. Any employee working a split shift must receive one meal for each consecutive period of hours worked.

OKLAHOMA WAGE & HOUR LAW

LAW. Oklahoma's Wage & Hour Law applies to employees eighteen (18) to sixty-five (65), except those working for employers with less than ten employees at any one location. However, if an employer with less than ten employees grosses more than $100,000.00 annually he is covered by Oklahoma's State Wage & Hour Law provisions. The Law does not apply to those employers covered by Federal Wage & Hour Law; to part-time employees working less than twenty-five (25) hours per week; to those under eighteen (18) who have not finished high school or vocational training; or to those under twenty-two (22) who are enrolled in high school, college, or a vocational training program.

MINIMUM WAGE. The minimum wage in Oklahoma is $1.85 per hour.

OVERTIME. Oklahoma's overtime provisions are sexually discriminatory and probably unenforceable.

In cases of emergency, hotel and restaurant employees are required to receive double time.

CREDITS. Credits for tips, meals, and lodging may be taken pursuant to Federal Wage & Hour Law.

Additionally, credits for the reasonable cost of uniforms may be taken.

Employers must furnish to the employee a written list of all credits taken.

EQUAL PAY. Equal pay for equivalent work, regardless of sex, is required.

CHILD LABOR LAW. No one under eighteen (18) may work in any capacity where alcoholic beverages of more than one-half of one percent alcohol by volume are sold for consumption on the premises, except in an establishment where such alcoholic sales do not exceed twenty-five (25%) of the gross receipts.

No one under fifteen (15) may work in any establishment where beer is served.

OREGON WAGE & HOUR LAW

LAW. Oregon's Wage & Hour Law is applicable to anyone over eighteen (18) years of age, except those individuals covered by Federal Wage & Hour Law.

MINIMUM WAGE. The minimum wage is $2.30 per hour. There is a special minimum pay schedule for camp counselors, and special rates may be set for handicapped workers by application to the Bureau of Labor.

OVERTIME. Overtime is required at the rate of time and one-half the regular rate for all hours over forty (40) within the workweek.

CREDITS. The fair market value of meals and other services may be credited toward the minimum wage. Uniforms, laundry costs, and breakage may not be credited.

Commissions may be credited toward the minimum wage due the worker in certain situations.

EQUAL PAY. Equal pay for equivalent work is required, regardless of sex.

CHILD LABOR LAW. Minimum wage rates and overtime rates are the same for minors as for adults.

No one under eighteen (18) may be employed where alcoholic beverages are sold for consumption on the premises, operate an elevator, or work more than forty-four (44) hours per week without a special emergency overtime permit. Work permits are required.

No one under sixteen (16) may work in a restaurant, hotel, business office, store, etc., without an employment certificate. They may not operate hazardous, power-driven machinery. Their hours are limited to ten (10) per day; six (6) days per week; from 7 a.m. to 6 p.m., except from 6 a.m. to 10 p.m. in an organized youth camp.

No one under fourteen (14) may be employed in a restaurant, hotel, store, etc., or in any place during the school term.

STRIKES AND EMERGENCIES. Wages due strikers must be paid on the next regular payday. In emergencies, hotel and restaurant employees must receive double time.

REST PERIOD. For each four (4) hours worked, an employee must be given a paid ten-minute (10) rest period.

PENNSYLVANIA WAGE & HOUR LAW

LAW. Pennsylvania's Wage & Hour Law is applicable to all nonsupervisory employees, except those in seasonal recreational establishments.

MINIMUM WAGE. The minimum wage is $2.30 an hour. Sub-minimum rates of eighty-five percent (85%) of the minimum wage may be paid to students and learners under special certificates.

OVERTIME. Effective May 1, 1977, hotel, motel, and restaurant employees must be paid time and one-half for all hours over forty (40) worked in the workweek. Employees in private clubs and other eating establishments have different rules.

CREDITS. Employers may take a fifty percent (50%) tip credit under rules similar to the Federal Wage & Hour Law.

Employers may also take food and lodging credits for the reasonable costs thereof.

Any other credits or deductions may be taken only as required by Law or specifically authorized by the employee for his/her benefit.

EQUAL PAY. Equal pay for equivalent work is required.

CHILD LABOR LAW. No one under eighteen (18) may sell or dispense alcoholic beverages for consumption on the premises.

Minors sixteen (16) to eighteen (18) may work in restaurants or hotels where alcoholic beverages are sold and served only in areas or capacities in which they do not serve or dispense alcoholic beverages, *e.g.*, serve food, clean tables, etc., provided food and nonalcoholic beverages constitute at least forty percent (40%) of the restaurant's gross receipts. Their hours are limited from 6 a.m. to 11 p.m., except to midnight if the next day is not a school day. They are limited to eight (8) hours per day, forty-four (44) hours and six (6) days per week, except to twenty-eight (28) hours per week when enrolled in school.

No one under sixteen (16) may be employed in any occupation, except that minors twelve (12) to fourteen (14) may be golf caddies, and minors fourteen (14) to sixteen (16) may do work which does not interfere with school attendance.

No one under sixteen (16) may work in any capacity in a restaurant where alcoholic beverages are sold. Their hours are limited from 7 a.m. to 7 p.m., except 7 a.m. to 10 p.m. between June 1 and Labor Day.

REST PERIOD. A rest or meal period of at least thirty (30) minutes must be provided employees for each five-hour (5) work period. Restaurant employees must complete their shifts within a thirteen-hour (13) period.

RHODE ISLAND WAGE & HOUR LAW

LAW. Rhode Island's Wage & Hour Law is applicable to all employees, except golf caddies; theatre ushers; shoeshine boys/girls; those working for a family member or as a minor in the employment of a parent; etc. Furthermore, Rhode Island's Minimum Wage Law is not applicable to seasonal resort foodservices between May 1 and October 1, which are not open for more than six (6) months of the year. In free-standing restaurants and in hotel restaurants where an employee's spread of hours in a day exceeds ten (10) or where there is more than one interval off duty (excluding a meal period of one hour or less), the employee shall receive an additional $.50 for the day. In resort hotels, restaurant employees shall receive the extra $.50 per day if the spread of hours exceeds twelve (12), or there are more than two intervals off duty (excluding any period of one hour or less). In all other hotel and motel jobs (public housekeeping), employees shall be paid an extra $.75 per day under such circumstances. Waiting time and travel time during working hours shall be counted as work time.

MINIMUM WAGE. The minimum wage is $2.30 an hour. Minors fourteen (14) and fifteen (15) may be paid $1.65 per hour for workweeks of less than 24 hours. If they work more than twenty-four (24) hours, they must be paid $2.30 per hour for all hours worked. Subminimum payments may be made to learners for a period no longer than ninety (90) days. Additionally, lower rates may be set for handicapped workers under special license from the Director of Labor.

OVERTIME. Time and one-half an employee's regular rate of pay is required for all hours over forty (40) in a workweek. Salaried employees making $200.00 a week or more, administrative and professional personnel, and summer camp personnel are exempt from overtime.

CREDITS. A tip credit of up to thirty-five percent (35%) of the employee's minimum wage may be taken; however, this tip credit provision is inapplicable to busboys/girls, unless they receive gratuities and tips directly from customers. Employers have the burden of proving that the employee receives the amount of tips for which a tip credit is being taken.

All other deductions are permitted only where required by Law or authorized by the employee for his/her benefit.

CHILD LABOR LAW. No one under twenty-one (21) may sell or serve alcoholic beverages for consumption on the premises, except for a wife or widow, daughters, or sisters of license holder (under Discrimination Laws, this probably applies to both sexes).

No one under eighteen (18) may work over nine (9) hours per day and forty-eight (48) hours per week, except that nine and three-fifths (9-3/5) may be worked in a day to make a five-day week. Hours are limited to those from 6 a.m. to 11 p.m.

No one under sixteen (16) may work with hazardous, power-driven equipment. Hours are limited to eight (8) per day and forty-eight (48) hours per week.

Minors fourteen (14) to sixteen (16) may work only between 6 a.m. and 7 p.m. Employment certificates are required for minors to work outside school hours.

No one under fourteen (14) may be employed in any business or industrial establishment.

SOUTH CAROLINA WAGE & HOUR LAW

LAW. There is no Wage & Hour Law in South Carolina.

MINIMUM WAGE. No provision.

OVERTIME. No provision.

CREDITS. Credits and deductions are permitted as required by Law or authorized by the employee for his/her benefit.

CHILD LABOR LAW. No one under twenty-one (21) may work in a retail liquor store. Bartenders must be twenty-one (21).

Persons over eighteen (18) may serve alcoholic beverages in restaurants, if the beverages are in sealed containers.

No one under sixteen (16) may work in restaurants where alcoholic beverages are sold for consumption on the premises.

No one under sixteen (16) may work after 8 p.m. on a day preceding a school day, or after 11 p.m. on other days.

WAGES DUE STRIKERS. Strikers must be paid at their next regular payday, including any other remuneration due the employee.

SOUTH DAKOTA WAGE & HOUR LAW

LAW. South Dakota's Wage & Hour Law applies to all employees eighteen (18) years of age and older.

MINIMUM WAGE. The minimum wage is $2.00 per hour, except that learners may be paid subminimum rates pursuant to published regulations.

OVERTIME. No provision.

CREDITS. Tip credits are not allowed in South Dakota, unless the employer specifically contracts with the employee to take a tip credit of not more than twenty-five percent (25%) of the minimum wage.

Meal and lodging credits may not be taken under South Dakota's Wage & Hour Law, unless a similar contract exists between the employee and the employer.

Other credits and deductions are permitted only as required by Law or requested by the employee for his/her benefit.

EQUAL PAY. Equal pay for equivalent work is required by South Dakota Law.

CHILD LABOR LAW. No one under eighteen (18) may serve low-point beer where such selling constitutes more than fifty percent (50%) of the gross receipts of the restaurant. No on-sale licensees may employ persons under twenty-one (21) years of age where alcoholic liquors are sold.

No one under sixteen (16) may work more than eight (8) hours per day and forty (40) hours per week.

No one under fourteen (14) may work except after school hours, and not at all after 7 p.m.

TENNESSEE WAGE & HOUR LAW

LAW. Tennessee does not have a Wage & Hour Law.

MINIMUM WAGE. No provision.

OVERTIME. No provision.

CREDITS. No provision.

EQUAL PAY. Equal pay for equivalent work is required by Tennessee Law.

CHILD LABOR LAW. No one under eighteen (18) may work where twenty-five percent (25%) of the monthly gross receipts come from the sale of alcoholic beverages, or where minors take orders for alcoholic beverages, or around hazardous, power-driven equipment. Hours of sixteen- (16) and seventeen-year-old (17) children are limited to ten (10) per day, forty-eight (48) per week, and six (6) days per week if not in school; and six (6) per day, thirty-six (36) per week when in school. They may work from 6 a.m. to 12 midnight, except only until 10 p.m. if enrolled in school and the next day is a school day.

No one under sixteen (16) may be employed in any occupation that would interfere with the minor's health, schooling, or well-being. Their hours are limited from 7 a.m. to 7 p.m., except to 9 p.m. between June 1 and Labor Day.

No one under fourteen (14) may be employed in any gainful occupation, except for errands and delivery work by foot, bicycle, or public transportation, and janitorial work in the parents' business. All minors must obtain employment certificates.

TEXAS WAGE & HOUR LAW

LAW. Texas' Wage & Hour Law is applicable to all employees, except those covered by the Federal Wage & Hour Law; those under eighteen (18) who have not finished high school or vocational school; those under twenty (20) who are students in high school, college, and vocational school; administrative and professional employees; and employees of certain amusement and recreational establishments, etc.

MINIMUM WAGE. The minimum wage is $1.40 per hour.

OVERTIME. No provision.

CREDITS. A tip credit may be taken up to fifty-percent (50%) of the minimum wage.

The reasonable cost of meals may also be credited. Other credits are permitted only where required by Law, or where specifically authorized by the employee.

CHILD LABOR LAW. No one under eighteen (18) may sell, handle, or dispense alcoholic beverages.

No one under fifteen (15) may work more than eight (8) hours per day and forty-eight (48) hours per week. They may not work from 10 p.m. to 5 a.m.

Children over fourteen (14) may secure work permits pursuant to certain hardship cases.

UTAH WAGE & HOUR LAW

LAW. Utah's Wage & Hour Law is probably inconsistent with Sex Discrimination Laws since it details specific provisions applicable to women and minors.

MINIMUM WAGE. Again, the minimum wage is applicable primarily to women and minors and is established in various zones varying from $1.70 to $1.85 per hour. Learners are permitted to be paid $.10 per hour less for the first eighty hours, and students may be paid subminimum rates of $.20 less than the minimum wage.

OVERTIME. No provision.

CREDITS. A tip credit of twenty-five percent (25%) of the minimum wage is allowed. A meal credit of fifty percent (50%) of the menu price of the meal may be taken.

Uniforms must be provided at no cost to the employees.

It is a crime (misdemeanor) for an employer not to comply with an employee's written request for a union dues checkoff up to a maximum of three percent (3%) per month of the employee's wages.

CHILD LABOR LAW. No one under eighteen (18) may work where alcoholic beverages are sold for consumption on the premises, or in any hazardous occupation.

No one under sixteen (16) may work during school hours without permission of school officials. Their hours are limited to eight (8) per day, forty (40) per week, except four (4) per day on school days if the next day is also a school day, and from 5 a.m. to 9:30 p.m.

Minors over fourteen (14) may work in nonhazardous occupations such as retail foodservice, janitorial work, lawn care, snow removal, etc.

SPLIT SHIFT AND MEAL PERIODS. Utah's Wage & Hour Law requires that a split shift be limited to two working periods within twelve consecutive hours. Further, the split-shift hours must not total more than eight (8). Rest and meal periods are required by Utah's Wage & Hour Law.

VERMONT WAGE & HOUR LAW

LAW. Vermont's Wage & Hour Law is applicable to employers with two or more employees, but it does not apply to students.

MINIMUM WAGE. The minimum wage is $2.30 per hour.

OVERTIME. Hotel, motel, and restaurant employees are exempt from the overtime provisions of Vermont's Wage & Hour Law. Where required, overtime must be paid for all hours over forty (40) in a workweek.

CREDITS. Tipped employees who regularly receive at least $20.00 a month in tips are subject to a tip allowance according to the following schedule. Service employees in hotels and restaurants must receive $1.50 per hour with a maximum tip credit of $.80; service employees in resort hotels must receive $1.30 with a maximum tip credit of $1.00; chambermaids in resort hotels must receive $1.75 per hour with a maximum tip credit of $.55; counter-service employees must receive $1.80 per hour with a maximum tip credit of $.50; and all nonservice employees must receive $2.30 per hour without a tip credit.

Service employee learners and trainees may be employed up to thirty (30) days at the following rates. In restaurants and hotels, the rate is $1.35 per hour with a maximum tip credit of $.95; and in resort hotels, $1.15 per hour with a maximum tip credit of $1.15.

A meal credit of $.85 per meal may be taken.

Room and board and lodging credits at the rate of $20.55 per week may be taken. Full board at the rate of $15.30 per week may be taken. Full room at the rate of $5.25 per week may be taken. Lodging may be credited at the rate of $.75 per night.

Uniforms must be provided by the employer.

CHILD LABOR LAW. No one under eighteen (18) may serve or dispense alcoholic beverages in an establishment holding a first- or third-class license (less than sixteen (16) for a second-class license). Hotel, restaurant, and club establishments holding a first- or third-class license may, with permission of the Liquor Control Board, allow minors sixteen (16) to eighteen (18) to entertain when accompanied by an adult.

No one under sixteen (16) may work with hazardous, power-driven equipment, or during school hours, without an employment certificate. Hours are limited to eight (8) per day, forty-eight (48) hours and six (6) days per week, and from 6 a.m. to 7 p.m.

No one under fourteen (14) may work at any gainful occupation during school hours.

VIRGINIA WAGE & HOUR LAW

LAW. Virginia's Wage & Hour Law is applicable to all employees, except those under eighteen (18) employed by a parent or guardian; minors under sixteen (16); employees over sixty-five (65); students; employers with four or fewer employees; minors under eighteen (18) in school full-time working less than twenty (20) hours per week; and all employees covered by the Federal Wage & Hour Law.

MINIMUM WAGE. The minimum wage is $2.35 per hour.

OVERTIME. No provision.

CREDITS. Tip credits are allowed under Virginia's Wage & Hour Law.
Likewise, meal and lodging credits are allowed.

EQUAL PAY. Equal pay for equivalent work is required by Virginia's Equal Pay Act.

CHILD LABOR LAW. No one under twenty-one may sell, serve, or dispense alcoholic beverages for consumption on the premises. They may not drive a public-passenger vehicle. Their hours are limited to eight (8) per day and forty (40) per week, and employment certificates are required.
No one under eighteen (18) may work in a place where alcoholic beverages are sold for consumption on the premises, except entertainers with a special permit from the Commissioner of Labor. They may not work with certain types of hazardous, power-driven equipment. Minors sixteen (16) and seventeen (17) may work until midnight.
No one under sixteen (16) may be employed as a lifeguard, in concessions at any hotel or motel pool, in hotel or motel room service, in the operation of any elevator, in any parking lot, or in a club or roadhouse.
With a permit, minors fourteen (14) and fifteen (15) may work until 10 p.m. on a night not preceding a school day; otherwise, they may work only between 7 a.m. and 6 p.m. Minors working outdoors, such as caddies, etc., may work between 6 a.m. and one-half hour before sunset.

WASHINGTON WAGE & HOUR LAW

LAW. Washington's Wage & Hour Law is applicable to all employees, except administrative, professional, and on-call employees, etc.

MINIMUM WAGE. The minimum wage is $2.30 an hour for food and beverage service employees. Minors under eighteen (18) may be paid $1.75 per hour. Learners may be paid eighty-five percent (85%) of the minimum wage and student learners at seventy-five percent (75%) of the minimum wage. Subminimum wage rates may also be paid handicapped workers commensurate with their earning capacities.

OVERTIME. Overtime is required at the rate of time and one-half for all hours over forty (40) worked within the workweek.

CREDITS. Tips may not be credited toward minimum wage obligations of an employer. Similarly, no deductions may be taken for cash shortages, walkouts, customer breakage, etc. Credits and deductions are allowed when authorized by Law or specifically authorized by the employee.

EQUAL PAY. Equal pay for equivalent work is required.

CHILD LABOR LAW. No one under twenty-one (21) may sell and serve mixed drinks in a bar or cocktail lounge, or sell beer and wine for consumption on the premises without the supervision of an adult over twenty-one (21). Employees eighteen (18) years of age and older working on the premises of a Class "A", "C", "D", and/or "H" licensee may serve and sell mixed drinks in all parts of the licensed premises, except the cocktail lounge and bar areas. Employees of a Class "A", "C", "D", and/or "H" licensee may enter the bar and cocktail lounge areas to pick up the mixed drinks for service in other parts of the restaurant and/or to clear and arrange tables in the bar and cocktail lounge sections.
In Classes "E" and "F" establishments, employees eighteen (18) years of age and older may sell wine and beer if there is a supervisor who is at least twenty-one (21) years old.
Professional musicians over eighteen (18) may work as musicians only in premises licensed to serve alcoholic beverages.
No one under eighteen (18) may work without a work permit or work as a maid or bellhop in a hotel and motel, unless the minor is accompanied by a responsible adult whenever work requires the minor to enter guest rooms. Their hours are limited to eight (8) per day, five days per week, and no later than 9 p.m. on a night preceding a school day.
No one under sixteen (16) may fillet fish; dress poultry; operate power-driven machinery; wash windows above ground level; do maintenance and repair work; work in boiler and engine rooms; operate and maintain power-driven food slicers, grinders, choppers, cutters, and bakery-type mixers; work in freezers and meat coolers; or load and unload trucks. They may not work during school hours without a permit. Their hours are limited to three (3) per day on school days; eighteen (18) per week during school weeks; 7 a.m. to 7 p.m. during school years; and 9 p.m. during summer vacations.

No one under fourteen (14) may be employed without the permission of a Superior Court Judge.

MEAL AND REST PERIODS. A meal period of at least thirty (30) minutes per eight (8) hours must be paid. Similarly, a rest period of at least ten (10) minutes off per four (4) hours of work is required.

WEST VIRGINIA WAGE & HOUR LAW

LAW. West Virginia's Wage & Hour Law is applicable to all employers with six or more employees during any calendar week. It is inapplicable to employers with eighty percent (80%) of his/her work force covered by the Federal Wage & Hour Law. Similarly, it does not cover those employees over sixty-two (62) who are receiving Social Security benefits, full-time students who work part time, employees of parents and spouses, and supervisory and professional employees.

MINIMUM WAGE. The minimum wage is $2.20 per hour.

OVERTIME. Overtime is required for all hours worked over forty-two (42) per week.

CREDITS. Tips may be credited up to twenty percent (20%) of the minimum wage. Meals may be credited up to $1.00 per day. Uniforms and uniform maintenance may not be credited or deducted. All deductions are allowed only where required by Law or requested by the employee.

EQUAL PAY. Equal pay for comparable work is required.

CHILD LABOR LAW. No one under eighteen (18) may be employed to sell, serve, or dispense beer if dancing is allowed in the same room.
No one under sixteen (16) may be employed without an employment permit. Their hours are limited to eight (8) per day, forty (40) per week, six (6) days per week, and between 5 a.m. to 8 p.m., except until 11 p.m. in concerts or theatrical performances. Minors must have a thirty-minute (30) lunch period after working continuously for five (5) hours.
No one under fifteen (15) may be employed to entertain in any place where alcoholic beverages are served.

WISCONSIN WAGE & HOUR LAW

LAW. Wisconsin's Wage & Hour Law covers all employees.

MINIMUM WAGE. The minimum wage is $2.20 per hour. It applies to all employees over eighteen (18) working more than fifteen (15) hours per week. Employees seventeen (17) and under may be paid $1.76 per hour. Students fourteen (14) to eighteen (18) and handicapped workers may be paid not less than seventy-five percent (75%) of the minimum wage under special permits. Caddies must be paid $2.75 per nine holes and $4.80 for eighteen holes.

OVERTIME. Overtime is required for all hours over forty-eight (48).

CREDITS. A tip credit of up to twenty-five percent (25%) of the minimum wage is allowed, provided the employer can prove that the credit is no more than the tips actually recieved.

Meal credits up to $1.25 per meal and $26.40 per week for employees over eighteen (18) may be taken. Employees seventeen (17) years of age and under are subject to a meal credit of $1.00 per meal and $21.10 per week.

A lodging credit up to $2.50 per day and $17.60 per week may be taken for employees eighteen (18) and over. Employees seventeen (17) years and under are subject to a lodging credit up to $2.00 per day and $14.10 per week.

Credits and deductions are not allowed for breakage and shortages, unless it is determined that the breakage and shortages were due to the negligence or willful act of the employee.

EQUAL PAY. Equal pay for equivalent work is required under Wisconsin's Wage & Hour Law.

CHILD LABOR LAW. No one under eighteen (18) may work during school hours, except for high school graduates and students in vocational training programs. Minors under eighteen (18) may not work where alcoholic beverages are sold for consumption on the premises, except that those over seventeen (17) may work in hotels, restaurants, etc., provided they do not handle or serve alcoholic beverages.

Minors under eighteen (18) may not work as lifeguards, except that those over sixteen (16) may do so with proper adult supervision. Their hours are limited to eight (8) per day, forty (40) per week, and six (6) days per week while school is in session, and to forty-eight (48) hours per week when school is not in session. Time and one-half for overtime up to a maximum total of fifty (50) hours per week is required. Their hours are limited to those from 6 a.m. to 12 p.m., except under adult supervision and provided that on days preceding school days, the minor receives at least eight consecutive hours of rest between the ending of work and beginning of school.

No one under sixteen (16) may operate hazardous, power-driven equipment or work in pool halls, dance halls, race tracks, etc. Their hours are limited to eight (8) per day, forty-eight (48) hours and six (6) days per week when school is in session; forty (40) hours per week when school is not in session; 7 a.m. to 8 p.m. on days preceding school days; and to 9:30 p.m. on days not preceding school days.

Minors fourteen (14) and over may work in restaurants and grounds keeping. They may not cook, other than at soda fountains, lunch counters, snack bars, and cafeteria serving counters. They are prohibited from operating and maintaining power-driven food slicers, grinders, choppers, and cutters; power lawn mowers; and other hazardous, power-driven machinery. They are also prohibited from washing windows above ground level.

Minors under fourteen (14) may not be employed, except that those over twelve (12) may work as golf caddies with a permit, in agriculture, and in "street trades."

WYOMING WAGE & HOUR LAW

LAW. Wyoming's Wage & Hour Law covers all employees eighteen (18) years of age and older, except those working twenty (20) hours or less per week, those doing piecework, and professional and administrative personnel.

MINIMUM WAGE. The minimum wage is $1.60 per hour.

OVERTIME. No provision.

CREDITS. A fifty percent (50%) tip credit may be taken under this provision, similar to that allowed under Federal Law. However, the base hourly wage of an employee must be at least $1.10 per hour.

CHILD LABOR LAW. No one under sixteen (16) may work without a work permit or where liquor is sold for consumption on the premises. On nights preceding school days, they may not work after 10 p.m.; on nights not preceding school days, they may work until midnight.

ALABAMA:

   Department of Industrial Relations
   Industrial Relations Building
   Montgomery, Alabama 36130

ALASKA:

   Director, Wage and Hour Division
   P.O. Box 1149
   Juneau, Alaska 99811

ARIZONA:

   Director, State Labor Department
   P.O. Box 19070
   Phoenix, Arizona 85012

ARKANSAS:

   Labor Standards Division
   Department of Labor
   Capital Hill Bldg.
   Little Rock, Arkansas 72201

CALIFORNIA:

   Division of Labor Standards Enforcement
   Department of Industrial Relations
   455 Golden Gate Avenue
   P.O. Box 603
   San Francisco, California 94101

DELAWARE:

   Department of Labor and
      Industrial Relations
   508 W. 10th Street
   Wilmington, Delaware 19801

DISTRICT OF COLUMBIA:

   Director of Minimum Wage Division
   North Potomac Building
   614 H Street, N.W., Room 615
   Washington, D.C. 20001

FLORIDA:

>Director of Labor
>1321 Executive Center Dr., E.
>200 Ashley Building
>Tallahassee, Florida 32301

GEORGIA:

>Department of Labor
>State Labor Building
>254 Washington St.
>Atlanta, Georgia 30334

HAWAII:

>Department of Labor and
>   Industrial Relations
>825 Miliani Street
>Honolulu, Hawaii 96813

IDAHO:

>Department of Labor and
>   Industrial Services
>317 Main Street, Room 400
>Statehouse
>Boise, Idaho 83702

ILLINOIS:

>Director, Illinois Department of Labor
>910 S. Michigan
>Chicago, Illinois 60605

INDIANA:

>Division of Labor
>Indiana State Office Building
>Room 1013
>100 N. Senate Avenue
>Indianapolis, Indiana 46204

IOWA:

> Bureau of Labor
> East 7th and Court Avenue
> Des Moines, Iowa 50319

KANSAS:

> Commissioner, Department of Labor
> 401 Topeka Avenue
> Topeka, Kansas 66603

KENTUCKY:

> Commissioner, Department of Labor
> Capitol Plaza Tower
> Frankfort, Kentucky 40601

LOUISIANA:

> Commissioner, Dept. of Labor
> 1045 Natural Resources Bldg.
> P.O. Box 44063
> Baton Rouge, Louisiana 70804

MAINE:

> Director, Bureau of Labor
> Department of Manpower Affairs
> State Office Building
> Augusta, Maine 04333

MARYLAND:

> Commissioner of Labor and Industry
> Department of Licensing and Regulation
> Division of Labor and Industry
> 203 E. Baltimore Street
> Baltimore, Maryland 21202

MASSACHUSETTS:

> Commissioner, Department of
>   Labor and Industries
> State Office Building
> 100 Cambridge Street
> Boston, Massachusetts 02202

MICHIGAN:

    Director, Michigan Dept. of Labor
    Department of Labor
    Leonard Plaza Bldg.
    309 N. Washington
    Lansing, Michigan 48909

MINNESOTA:

    Commissioner
    Department of Labor and Industry
    444 Lafayette Rd.
    St. Paul, Minnesota 55101

MISSISSIPPI:

    Director
    Occupational Safety and Health Division
    Mississippi State Board of Health
    2628 Southerland Street
    Jackson, Mississippi 39216

MISSOURI:

    Division of Labor Standards
    Department of Labor and
      Industrial Relations
    722 Jefferson St.
    P.O. Box 449
    Jefferson City, Missouri 65101

MONTANA:

    Commissioner
    Department of Labor and Industry
    1331 Helena Avenue
    Helena, Montana 59601

NEBRASKA:

    Commissioner of Labor
    Department of Labor
    Box 94600
    State House Station
    Lincoln, Nebraska 68509

NEVADA:

> State Labor Commissioner
> Nevada State Labor Commission
> Capitol Complex
> Carson City, Nevada 89710

NEW HAMPSHIRE:

> Labor Commissioner
> Department of Labor
> 1 Pillsbury Street
> Concord, New Hampshire 03301

NEW JERSEY:

> Commissioner
> Department of Labor and Industry
> John Fitch Plaza
> P.O. Box V
> Trenton, New Jersey 08625

NEW MEXICO:

> Chief Deputy Labor Commissioner
> Wage and Hour
> 608 North Main Street
> Carlsbad, New Mexico 88220

NEW YORK (CITY):

> New York Office
> 2 World Trade Center
> New York, New York 10047

NEW YORK (STATE):

> Industrial Commissioner
> Department of Labor
> Building 12, State Campus
> Albany, New York 12240

NORTH CAROLINA:

> Director
> Division of State Inspections
>   and Services
> Raleigh, North Carolina 27611

Commissioner
Department of Labor
Labor Bldg.
P.O. Box 27407
Raleigh, North Carolina 27611

NORTH DAKOTA:

Commissioner of the Department
    of Labor
State Capitol
Bismarck, North Dakota 58501

OHIO:

Director
Department of Industrial Relations
2323 W. 5th Avenue
Columbus, Ohio 43216

OKLAHOMA:

Commissioner
Department of Labor
State Capitol
Oklahoma City, Oklahoma 73105

OREGON:

Commissioner
Bureau of Labor
473 State Office Bldg.
Portland, Oregon 97201

PENNSYLVANIA:

Director
Bureau of Labor Standards
Department of Labor and Industry
Labor and Industry Building
Harrisburg, Pennsylvania 17120

PUERTO RICO:

Puerto Rico Department of Labor
414 Barbosa Avenue
Hato Rey, Puerto Rico

RHODE ISLAND:

> Administrator, Labor Standards
> Department of Labor
> 235 Promenade Street
> Providence, Rhode Island 02908

SOUTH CAROLINA:

> Commissioner
> Department of Labor
> 3600 Forest Dr.
> P.O. Box 11329
> Columbia, South Carolina 29201

SOUTH DAKOTA:

> Director
> Department of Labor
> Division of Labor and Management
> Foss Building, Room 425
> Pierre, South Dakota 57501

TENNESSEE:

> Commissioner
> Department of Labor
> 501 Union Bldg., Second Floor
> Nashville, Tennessee 37219

TEXAS:

> Commissioner
> Department of Labor and Standards
> P.O. Box 12157, Capitol Station
> Austin, Texas 78711

UTAH:

> Industrial Commission of Utah
> Minimum Wage Division
> 350 East 5th South
> Salt Lake City, Utah 84111

VERMONT:

> Commissioner
> Department of Labor and Industry
> Montpelier, Vermont 05602

VIRGINIA:

> Commissioner
> Department of Labor and Industry
> P.O. Box 1814
> Ninth Street Office Bldg.
> Richmond, Virginia 23214

WASHINGTON:

> Director
> Department of Labor and Industries
> General Administration Building
> Olympia, Washington 98504

WEST VIRGINIA:

> Commissioner
> Department of Labor
> Room B-451
> 1900 Washington St., East
> Charleston, West Virginia 25305

WISCONSIN:

> Department of Industry, Labor and
>   Human Relations
> 201 East Washington Ave., Room 401
> Madison, Wisconsin 53702

WYOMING:

> Commissioner of Labor
> Department of Labor and Statistics
> Barrett Bldg., 4th Floor
> Cheyenne, Wyoming 82002

APPENDIX C

STATE
WAGE & HOUR LAW
SELECTED
POSTERS
AND
DOCUMENTS

INDUSTRIAL WELFARE COMMISSION

1976 Wage Orders

When people ask about California's "wage orders," they mean the orders adopted by the Industrial Welfare Commission, effective October 18, 1976.

The fifteen different Industrial Welfare Commission (IWC) orders establish the minimum standards for wages, hours, and working conditions for employees in twelve different industries and in three groups of occupations not otherwise covered by industry orders. In general they protect all non-managerial employees in California, except those working for government agencies or as outside salespersons, or those engaged in activities like on-site construction, on-site drilling and mining, or on-site logging.

Each IWC order is a separate section of Title 8 of the California Administrative Code and has full force of law, with appropriate penalties for violation. Each is printed in poster form which must be displayed where employees can read it, or which, in private households, must be kept available to employees on request.

The minimum wage is the same in all orders, and the sections regulating working conditions are basically the same with minor variations. It is practical, therefore, to review the orders section by section. But the orders DO vary considerably with regard to special conditions affecting overtime pay, so it is important to know which order protects the employee. The applicable order is determined not so much by the occupation of the employee as it is by the main business of the employer.

State of California, Agriculture and Services Agency, Department of Industrial Relations
DIVISION OF LABOR STANDARDS ENFORCEMENT

Summary of Basic Provisions

Applicability and Definitions: The question of whether management employees are exempt from overtime is often at issue, so tests for exempt administrative, executive, or professional jobs, stated in Section 1, Applicability of Order, are important. They include a description of the duties and a requirement that monthly wages of the employee be at least \$720.

The coverage of the order is described in detail in Definitions (Section 2). Other definitions have an important effect on enforcement, such as the new ones, "workday" and "workweek," which are necessary in the calculation of overtime. Special problems of a particular industry may be reflected in this section: orders covering beauticians, for example, expand the definition of "employee" to deal with the problem that booth renters are often misrepresented as independent contractors and thus deprived of protection.

Hours and Days of Work: Section 3 re-establishes the basic *eight-hour day* that previously applied only to women in California, not as a limit on the time that can be worked—most such limits have been dropped—but as the starting point for computing overtime, at one and one-half the regular rate of pay. This fundamental provision also includes *double time after 12 hours* in a workday and after the first eight hours on the seventh working day of the workweek.

The new order for *Household Occupations* applies this eight-hour day to employees who do live in. Detailed requirements for off-duty time for live-in employees result in overtime after nine hours of work in a day. (Personal attendants, including baby sitters, are not covered by this order.)

Workers in *Agricultural Occupations* are to be paid time-and-one-half after *ten hours* in a day and after *six days* in a week. Double time is payable after the first eight hours on the seventh day of work in a week.

In all but the agricultural and household orders, an alternate method of computing overtime is allowed, based on not more than *four days of work or not more than ten hours each*. These four days must be regularly scheduled, within five consecutive days.

1976 Orders by Title

1-76. Manufacturing Industry
2-76. Personal Service Industry
3-76. Canning, Freezing, and Preserving Industry
4-76. Professional, Technical, Clerical, Mechanical and Similar Occupations
5-76. Public Housekeeping Industry
6-76. Laundry, Linen Supply, Dry Cleaning, and Dyeing Industry
7-76. Mercantile Industry
8-76. Industries Handling Products after Harvest
9-76. Transportation Industry
10-76. Amusement and Recreation Industry
11-76. Broadcasting Industry
12-76. Motion Picture Industry
13-76. Industries Preparing Agricultural Products for Market, on the Farm
14-76. Agricultural Occupations
15-76. Household Occupations

and must be adopted in advance by a written voluntary agreement between the employer and at least two-thirds of the affected employees. A person on such a schedule who works overtime is paid time-and-one-half for the eleventh and twelfth hours in the workday, and double time after that. An employee who is called in to work on any additional day in the workweek must be paid time-and-one-half for the first eight hours and double time after that.

In the three orders covering canning and packing industries, there is a 72-hour limit on the time an employee can work during a workweek. The Public Housekeeping Order makes special provisions for hospitals and group homes. The Motion Picture Industry Order has embellishments of its own. Specialized groups of employees, including drivers in interstate commerce, are exempted from overtime requirements in a few orders.

A significant exception to about half the orders provides that a collective bargaining agreement which includes any provision for overtime at all shall prevail over the Hours section of the order. This appears in orders covering the manufacturing, laundry, mercantile, transportation, broadcasting, motion picture industries, and in Order 4-76, covering Professional, Technical, Clerical, Mechanical, and Similar Occupations. It does NOT appear in orders covering personal service, public housekeeping, canning, packing, or amusement and recreation industries, or in the orders protecting employees in agricultural or household occupations.

Other Hours provisions include curfews for minors and a requirement that workers on graveyard shift must have facilities available for hot food or drink.

The Minimum Wage is established in Section 4 of each order. In this order there is a \$2.50 per hour. Two exceptions are allowed under certain conditions: "Learners" may be paid \$2.15 per hour for the first 160 hours in an occupation in which they have had no previous related experience. Minors (under 18) may be paid \$2.15 provided that not more than 25 percent of the employees are paid at the lesser rate for minors. That limit is waived during extended school vacations.

This section also provides for payment of a split shift premium of \$2.50 per day in addition to the minimum wage.

Reporting Time: Section 5 basically says that if an employee is required to report to work but is furnished less than half the usual day's work, or none at all, the employee must be paid for half a day at the regular rate of pay, and in no case for less than two hours or more than four hours.

Permits and Licenses for Handicapped Workers: There is a section allowing special wage rates for persons so severely handicapped that they cannot approach normal production.

Records: Section 7 spells out the time and payroll information employers must keep to enable the Division of Labor Standards Enforcement to enforce the Industrial Welfare Commission regulations. These include a record of when the employee begins and ends each work period and when time is taken for meals.

Cash Shortage and Breakage: This was one of the protective regulations which had long been accepted in its application to women and which underwent some change in being extended to men. Employers may not make any deduction from wages unless the shortage or breakage is caused by a dishonest or willful act or by gross negligence. However, if the employee has exclusive and personal control of cash, the employer may require reimbursement for shortages, provided there are reasonable accounting procedures.

Uniforms and Equipment is becoming known as the "tools" section because of its most dramatic effect in its extension to men. Section 9 provides, first, that uniforms required on the job shall be paid for by the employer. Similarly, required hand tools and equipment must be furnished by the employer. An exception is made in the case of crafts and trades in which employees have customarily furnished their own tools, but only if such employees make at least twice the minimum wage. Employers may require a reasonable deposit for tools or uniforms furnished, refundable upon return of items.

Meals and Lodging may be used as credit against the minimum wage only with the employer's written agreement and certain other restrictions. The maximum amounts that may be so credited for breakfast, lunch, and dinner, are 90 cents, \$1.25, and \$1.65, respectively.

Meal and Rest Periods are covered in two sections. Basically an employee working a full day must have a 30-minute off-duty meal period, and all employees are entitled to ten minutes' rest time for every four hours (or major fraction) of work.

Change Rooms and Resting Facilities: All orders, except those for agricultural or household occupations, require lockers or closets for employees' outer clothing and change rooms where a change of clothing is needed on the job. The former requirement that a specified number of couches be available to women has been replaced by this language: "Suitable resting facilities shall be provided in an area separate from the toilet rooms and shall be available to employees during work hours."

Seats are required where the job permits the use of seats, and employees who have to stand at work are to have a place nearby where they can sit when there are lulls in operations.

Temperature: Employers must use all feasible means to reduce excessive heat or humidity caused by the work process. They must also provide warm-up rooms for employees who work where temperatures are under 60°F.

Elevators, escalators, or similar service shall be provided for employees who have four floors or more above or below ground level.

Sections affecting physical premises were left out of the order covering private households and, in some cases, out of the agricultural order.

Lifting: Unwilling either to continue a flat limit on the number of pounds an employer can require an employee to lift or to leave a vacuum in this area, the IWC related permissible lifts to the employee's reasonable physical capability and to the usual requirements of the job. The section's most predictable effect is to assure that employees are informed of lifting requirements of a job when they are hired.

Closing sections relate to enforcement. These include the right of the Division of Labor Standards Enforcement to make inspections and its authority to grant exemptions from some sections, the requirement for posting the order, and the "Separability" provision that if any section is held invalid, the others will continue in force.

ORDER 5-76
Title 8, Calif. Administrative Code 11380

Replacing former Orders 5-68 and 1-74

Effective October 18, 1976

INDUSTRIAL WELFARE COMMISSION ORDER NO. 5-76, REGULATING WAGES, HOURS, AND WORKING CONDITIONS IN THE PUBLIC HOUSEKEEPING INDUSTRY

ORDER 5-76
PUBLIC HOUSEKEEPING

TO WHOM IT MAY CONCERN:

TAKE NOTICE: That pursuant to the Legislature's 1973 mandate to the Industrial Welfare Commission to review, update and promulgate regulations necessary to provide adequate and reasonable wages, hours, and working conditions appropriate for all employees, and by virtue of authority vested in the Commission by Sections 1171 through 1204 of the Labor Code of the State of California, and after investigation and findings pursuant to Section 1178 and after receiving recommendations from duly appointed wage boards, and after consideration of all written material and information submitted, and after public hearings duly held, notice of said hearings having been duly given in the manner provided by law, the Industrial Welfare Commission, upon its own motion has found and concluded that its Public Housekeeping Industry Order, Number 5-68, enacted on September 26, 1967 and its Minimum Wage Order 1-74 enacted on January 1, 1974, should be altered and amended.

NOW, THEREFORE, the Industrial Welfare Commission of the State of California does hereby alter and amend said Public Housekeeping Industry Order, Number 5-68, and its Minimum Wage Order 1-74.

1. APPLICABILITY OF ORDER

This Order shall apply to all persons employed in the public housekeeping industry whether paid on a time, piece rate, commission, or other basis, except that:

(A) The provisions of this Order shall not apply to student nurses in a school accredited by the California Board of Nursing Education and Nurse Registration or by the Board of Vocational Nurse and Psychiatric Technician Examiners or exempted by the provisions of Sections 2789 or 2884 of the Business and Professions Code;

(B) Provisions of Sections 3 through 12 shall not apply to persons employed in administrative, executive, or professional capacities. No person shall be considered to be employed in an administrative, executive or professional capacity unless one of the following conditions prevails:

(1) The employee is engaged in work which is primarily intellectual, managerial, or creative, and which requires exercise of discretion and independent judgment, and for which the remuneration is not less than $720.00 per month; or

(2) The employee is licensed or certified by the State of California and is engaged in the practice of one of the following recognized professions: law, medicine, dentistry, optometry, architecture, engineering, teaching, or accounting.

(C) The provisions of this Order shall not apply to employees directly employed by the State or any county, incorporated city or town or other municipal corporation, or to outside salespersons.

(D) Provisions of this Order shall not apply to any individual who is the parent, spouse, child, or legally adopted child of the employer.

2. DEFINITIONS

(A) "Commission" means the Industrial Welfare Commission of the State of California.

(B) "Division" means the Division of Labor Standards Enforcement of the State of California.

(C) "Public Housekeeping Industry" means any industry, business, or establishment which provides meals, housing, or maintenance services whether operated as a primary business or when incidental to other operations in an establishment not covered by an industry order of the Commission, and includes, but is not limited to the following:

(1) Restaurants, night clubs, taverns, bars, cocktail lounges, lunch counters, cafeterias, boarding houses, clubs, and all similar establishments where food in either solid or liquid form is prepared and served to be consumed on the premises;

(2) Catering, banquet, box lunch service, and similar establishments which prepare food for consumption on or off the premises;

(3) Hotels, motels, apartment houses, rooming houses, camps, clubs, trailer parks, office or loft buildings, and similar establishments offering rental of living, business, or commercial quarters;

State of California
Agriculture and Services Agency
Department of Industrial Relations

DIVISION OF LABOR STANDARDS ENFORCEMENT

Administrative headquarters:
P.O. Box 603, San Francisco 94101

District offices:
225 Chester Ave., Bakersfield 93301
1290 Howard Ave., Burlingame 94010
380 North 8th St., El Centro 92243
619 Second St., Eureka 95501
2550 Mariposa St., Fresno 93721
520 North La Brea Ave., Inglewood 90302
230 East 4th St., Long Beach 90812
107 South Broadway, Los Angeles 90012
1111 Jackson St., Oakland 94607
8155 Van Nuys Blvd., Panorama City 91402
300 South Park Ave., Pomona 91769
2115 Akard Ave., Redding 96001
2422 Arden Way, Sacramento 95825
21 West Laurel Drive, Salinas 93901
303 West 3rd St., San Bernardino 92401
1350 Front St., San Diego 92101
455 Golden Gate Ave., San Francisco 94102
888 North 1st St., San Jose 95112
28 Civic Center Plaza, Santa Ana 92701
411 East Canon Perdido, Santa Barbara 93101
725 Farmers Lane, Santa Rosa 95405
31 East Channel St., Stockton 95202
600 Marin St., Vallejo 94590

this Section by adopting, pursuant to a written agreement or understanding voluntarily arrived at between the employer and the employee before performance of the work, a work period of fourteen (14) consecutive workdays in lieu of a workweek of seven (7) consecutive days for purposes of overtime computation; provided that the employee shall be compensated for hours worked in excess of eight (8) hours in any workday and in excess of eighty (80) hours in any such fourteen (14) day work period at the rate of not less than one and one-half ($1\frac{1}{2}$) times the employee's regular rate of pay.

(D) This section shall not apply to employees eighteen (18) years of age or over who have direct responsibility for children under eighteen (18) years of age receiving twenty-four (24) hour care, nor to organized camp counselors, nor to resident managers of homes for the aged having less than eight (8) beds; provided that persons employed in such occupations shall not be employed more than fifty-four (54) hours nor more than six (6) days in any one workweek, except under the following conditions:

In case of emergency, employees eighteen (18) years of age or over may be employed in excess of fifty-four (54) hours or six (6) days in any one workweek provided the employee is compensated for all hours in excess of fifty-four (54) hours and six (6) days in one workweek at not less than one and one-half ($1\frac{1}{2}$) times the employee's regular rate of pay.

(E) No minor shall be employed more than eight (8) hours in any one day or more than six (6) days in any one week. One and one-half ($1\frac{1}{2}$) times the minor's regular rate of pay shall be paid for all work over forty (40) hours in any one week. No minor shall be employed before 5 o'clock in the morning or after 10 o'clock in the evening, except that during any evening preceding a non-school day a minor may work the hours authorized by this section until 12:30 o'clock in the morning of such non-school day.

(F) Minors sixteen (16) years of age or older and under the age of

be granted only upon joint application of employer and employee and employee's representative if any.

A special license may be issued to a nonprofit organization such as a sheltered workshop or rehabilitation facility fixing special minimum rates to enable the employment of such persons without requiring individual permits of such employees.

All such permits and licenses shall be renewed on a yearly basis or more frequently at the discretion of the Division.

See California Labor Code, Sections 1191 and 1191.5.

7. RECORDS

(A) Every employer shall keep accurate information with respect to each employee including the following:

(1) Full name, home address, occupation and social security number.

(2) Birthdate, if under 18 years, and designation as a minor.

(3) Time records showing when the employee begins and ends each work period. Meal periods, split shift intervals and total daily hours worked shall also be recorded. Meal periods during which operations cease and authorized rest periods need not be recorded.

(4) Total wages paid each payroll period, including value of board, lodging, or other compensation actually furnished to the employee.

(5) Total hours worked in the payroll period.

(6) When a piece rate or incentive plan is in operation, piece rates or an explanation of the incentive plan formula shall be provided to employees. An accurate production record shall be maintained by the employer.

(B) Every employer shall semimonthly or at the time of each payment of wages furnish each employee either as a detachable part of the check, draft, or voucher paying the employee's wages, or separately, an itemized statement in writing showing: (1) all deductions; (2) the inclusive dates of the period for which the employee is paid; (3) the name of the employee or the employee's social security number; and (4) the name of the employer; provided, all deductions made on written orders of the employee may be aggregated and shown as one item.

(C) All required records shall be in the English language and in ink or other indelible form, properly dated, showing month, day and year, and shall be kept on file by the employer for at least three years at the place of employment or at a central location within the State of California. An employee's records shall be available for inspection by the employee upon reasonable request.

(D) Clocks shall be provided in all major work areas or within reasonable distance thereto insofar as practicable.

8. CASH SHORTAGE AND BREAKAGE

Subject to the requirements of Sections 400–410 of the California Labor Code, no employer shall make any deduction from the wage or require any reimbursement from an employee for any cash shortage, breakage, or loss of equipment, unless it can be shown that the shortage, breakage, or loss is caused by a dishonest or willful act, or by the gross negligence of the employee. Notwithstanding the foregoing provision, where an employee has the exclusive and personal control of cash funds of the employer and is required by the employer to account, under reasonable accounting procedures, for said funds, the employer may upon prior written notice require reimbursement from such employee for cash shortages.

9. UNIFORMS AND EQUIPMENT

(A) When uniforms are required by the employer to be worn by the employee as a condition of employment, such uniforms shall be provided and maintained by the employer. The term "uniform" includes wearing apparel and accessories of distinctive design or color.

(B) When tools or equipment are required by the employer or are necessary to the performance of a job, such tools and equipment shall be provided and maintained by the employer, except that an employee whose wages are at least two (2) times the minimum wage provided herein may be required to provide and maintain hand tools and equipment customarily required by the trade or craft. Notwithstanding any other provision of this section, employees in beauty salons, schools of beauty culture offering beauty care to the public for a fee, and barber shops may be required to furnish their own manicure implements, curling irons, rollers, clips, hair-cutting scissors,

13. CHANGE ROOMS AND RESTING FACILITIES

(A) Employers shall provide suitable lockers, closets, or equivalent for the safekeeping of employees' outer clothing during working hours, and when required, for their work clothing during nonworking hours. When the occupation requires a change of clothing, change rooms or equivalent space shall be provided where employees may change their clothing in reasonable privacy and comfort. These rooms or spaces may be adjacent to but shall be separate from toilet rooms and shall be kept clean and sanitary.

(B) Suitable resting facilities shall be provided in an area separate from the toilet rooms and shall be available to employees during work hours.

14. SEATS

(A) All working employees shall be provided with suitable seats when the nature of the work reasonably permits the use of seats.

(B) When employees are not engaged in the active duties of their employment and the nature of the work requires standing, an adequate number of suitable seats shall be placed in reasonable proximity to the work area and employees shall be permitted to use such seats.

15. TEMPERATURE

(A) The temperature maintained in each work area shall provide reasonable comfort consistent with industry-wide standards for the nature of the process and the work performed.

(B) If excessive heat or humidity is created by the work process, the employer shall take all feasible means to reduce such excessive heat or humidity to a degree providing reasonable comfort. Where the nature of the employment requires a temperature of less than 60° F., a heated room shall be provided to which employees may retire for warmth and such room shall be maintained at not less than 68°.

(C) A temperature of not less than 68° shall be maintained in the toilet rooms, resting rooms, and change rooms during hours of use.

16. ELEVATORS

Adequate elevator, escalator or similar service consistent with industry-wide standards for the nature of the process and the work performed shall be provided when employees are employed four floors or more, either above or below ground level.

17. LIFTING

No employee shall be required to lift, push, or carry any object which is beyond the employee's reasonable physical capability at any given time, except that it shall not be a violation of this section to require an employee to lift, push, or carry any object when such activity constitutes part of the usual duties of the job for which the employee was hired, or when it is specified in a classification or description of the job for which the employee was hired.

18. EXEMPTIONS

If, in the opinion of the Division after due investigation, it is found that the enforcement of any provision contained in Section 7, Records; Section 11, Meal Periods; Section 12, Rest Periods; Section 13, Change Rooms and Resting Facilities; Section 14, Seats; Section 15, Temperature; or Section 16, Elevators, would not materially affect the welfare or comfort of employees and would work an undue hardship on the employer, exemption may be made at the discretion of the Division. Such exemptions shall be in writing to be effective and may be revoked after reasonable notice is given in writing. Application for exemption shall be made by the employer or by the employee and/or the employee's representative to the Division in writing. A copy of the application shall be posted at the place of employment at the time the application is filed with the Division.

19. FILING REPORTS

Every employer shall furnish to the Commission and to the Division at all reasonable times any and all reports for information which may be required to carry out the purpose of this Order, such reports and information to be verified if and when so requested.

(4) Hospitals, sanitariums, rest homes, child nurseries, child care institutions, homes for the aged, and similar establishments offering board or lodging in addition to medical, surgical, nursing, convalescent, aged, or child care;
(5) Private schools, colleges, or universities, and similar establishments which provide board or lodging in addition to educational facilities;
(6) Establishments contracting for development, maintenance or cleaning of grounds; maintenance or cleaning of facilities and/or quarters of commercial units and living units; and
(7) Establishments providing veterinary or other animal care services.

(D) "Employ" means to engage, suffer, or permit to work.

(E) "Employee" means any person employed by an employer, and includes any lessee who is charged rent, or who pays rent for a chair, booth, or space and (1) who does not use his or her own funds to purchase requisite supplies, and (2) who does not maintain an appointment book separate and distinct from that of the establishment in which the space is located, and (3) who does not have a business license where applicable.

(F) "Employer" means any person as defined in Section 18 of the Labor Code, who directly or indirectly, or through an agent or any other person, employs or exercises control over the wages, hours, or working conditions of any person.

(G) "Hours worked" means the time during which an employee is subject to the control of an employer, and includes all the time the employee is suffered or permitted to work, whether or not required to do so, and in the case of an employee who is required to reside on the employment premises, that time spent carrying out assigned duties shall be counted as hours worked.

(H) "Minor" means, for the purpose of this Order, any person under the age of eighteen (18) years.

(I) "Outside Salesperson" means any person, 18 years of age or over, who customarily and regularly works more than half the working time away from the employer's place of business selling tangible or intangible items or obtaining orders or contracts for products, services or use of facilities.

• (J) "Split shift" means a work schedule which is interrupted by nonpaid nonworking periods established by the employer, other than bona fide rest or meal periods.

(K) "Teaching" means, for the purpose of Section 1 of this Order, the profession of teaching under a certificate from the Commission for Teacher Preparation and Licensing or teaching in an accredited college or university.

(L) "Wages" means all amounts paid for labor performed by employees of every description, whether the amount is fixed or ascertained by the standard of time, task, piece, commission basis or other method of calculation.

(M) "Workday" means any consecutive 24 hours beginning at the same time each calendar day.

(N) "Workweek" means any seven (7) consecutive days, starting with the same calendar day each week. "Workweek" is a fixed and regularly recurring period of 168 hours, seven (7) consecutive 24-hour periods.

3. HOURS AND DAYS OF WORK

(A) No employee eighteen (18) years of age or over shall be employed more than eight (8) hours in any one workday or more than forty (40) hours in any one workweek unless the employee receives one and one-half (1½) times such employee's regular rate of pay for all hours worked over forty (40) hours in the workweek. Employment beyond eight (8) hours in any one workday or more than six (6) days in any one workweek is permissible provided the employee is compensated for such overtime at not less than:
(1) One and one-half (1½) times the employee's regular rate of pay for all hours worked in excess of eight (8) hours up to and including twelve (12) hours in any one workday, and for the first eight (8) hours worked on the seventh (7th) workday; and
(2) Double the employee's regular rate of pay for all hours worked in excess of twelve (12) hours in any one workday and for all hours worked in excess of eight (8) hours on the seventh (7th) workday in any one workweek.

(B) No employer shall be deemed to have violated the provisions of the above subsection (A) by instituting, pursuant to a written agreement voluntarily executed by the employer and at least two-thirds (⅔) of the affected employees before the performance of the work, a regularly scheduled week of work which includes not more than four (4) working days of not more than ten (10) hours each within five (5) consecutive workdays, provided that:
(1) The employer is not required to pay the premium wage rate prescribed in subsection (A) for the 9th and 10th hours worked during such workdays;
(2) If an employee on such a four-day schedule is required or permitted to work more than ten (10) hours in any workday, the premium wage rate provisions in subsection (A) above shall apply to such employee for those hours worked in excess of the 10th hour of that work day;
(3) Any employee on such a schedule who is required or permitted to work on more than four (4) workdays shall be compensated at the rate of not less than one and one-half (1½) times the employee's regular rate of pay for the first eight (8) hours on such additional workdays and double the employee's regular rate of pay for work in excess of eight (8) hours on those workdays.

(C) No employer engaged in the operation of a licensed acute care or extended care hospital shall be deemed to have violated any provision of eighteen (18) years enrolled in work experience education programs approved by the State Department of Education may work after 10 p.m. but not later than 12:30 a.m. providing such employment is not detrimental to the health, education or welfare of the minors and the approval of the parent and the work experience coordinator has been obtained. However, any such minor who works any time during the hours from 10 p.m. to 12:30 a.m. shall be paid for work during that time at a rate which is not less than the minimum wage required for adults.

VIOLATIONS OF CHILD LABOR LAWS are subject to civil penalties of from $100 to $5,000 as well as to criminal penalties provided herein. Refer to California Labor Code Sections 1285 to 1311 and 1390 to 1398 for additional restrictions on the employment of minors.

(G) An employee may be employed on seven (7) workdays in one workweek with no overtime pay required when the total hours of employment during such workweek do not exceed thirty (30) and the total hours of employment in any one workday thereof do not exceed six (6).

(H) If a meal period occurs on a shift beginning or ending at or between the hours of 10 p.m. and 6 a.m., facilities shall be available for securing hot food or drink or for heating food or drink; and a suitable sheltered place shall be provided in which to consume such food or drink.

(I) The provisions of this section are not applicable to employees whose hours of service are regulated by the United States Department of Transportation Code of Federal Regulations, Title 49, sections 395.1 to 395.13, Hours of Service of Drivers.

(J) The daily overtime provisions of subsection (A) above shall not apply to ambulance drivers and attendants scheduled for twenty-four (24) hour shifts of duty who have agreed in writing to exclude from daily time worked not more than three (3) meal periods of not more than one hour each and a regularly scheduled uninterrupted sleeping period of not more than eight (8) hours. The employer shall provide adequate dormitory and kitchen facilities for employees on such a schedule.

4. MINIMUM WAGES

(A) Every employer shall pay to each employee wages not less than two dollars and fifty cents ($2.50) per hour for all hours worked, except:
(1) LEARNERS. Employees during their first one hundred and sixty (160) hours of employment in occupations in which they have no previous similar or related experience, for whom the rate of pay shall be not less than two dollars and fifteen cents ($2.15) per hour.
(2) MINORS may be paid two dollars and fifteen cents ($2.15) per hour; provided that the number of minors employed at said lesser rate shall not exceed twenty-five percent (25%) of the persons regularly employed in the establishment. An employer of less than ten (10) persons may employ three (3) minors at said lesser rate. The twenty-five percent (25%) limitation on the employment of minors shall not apply during school vacations.

(B) Every employer shall pay to each employee, on the established payday for the period involved, not less than the applicable minimum wage for all hours worked in the payroll period, whether the remuneration is measured by time, piece, commission, or otherwise.

(C) On any workday in which an employee works a split shift two dollars and fifty cents ($2.50) per workday shall be paid in addition to the minimum wage except when the employee resides at the place of employment.

(D) The provisions of this section shall not apply to apprentices regularly indentured under the State Division of Apprenticeship Standards.

5. REPORTING TIME PAY

(A) Each workday an employee is required to report for work and does report, but is not put to work or is furnished less than half said employee's usual or scheduled day's work, the employee shall be paid for half the usual or scheduled day's work, but in no event for less than two (2) hours nor more than four (4) hours, at the employee's regular rate of pay, which shall not be less than the minimum wage herein provided.

(B) If an employee is required to report for work a second time in any one workday and is furnished less than two hours of work on the second reporting, said employee shall be paid for two hours at the employee's regular rate of pay, which shall not be less than the minimum wage herein provided.

(C) The foregoing reporting time pay provisions are not applicable when:
(1) Operations cannot commence or continue due to threats to employees or property; or when recommended by civil authorities; or
(2) Public utilities fail to supply electricity, water, or gas, or there is a failure in the public utilities, or sewer system; or
(3) The interruption of work is caused by an Act of God or other cause not within the employer's control.

(D) This section shall not apply to an employee on paid standby status who is called to perform assigned work at a time other than the employee's scheduled reporting time.

6. PERMITS AND LICENSES FOR HANDICAPPED WORKERS

A permit may be issued by the Division authorizing employment of a person whose earning capacity is impaired by physical disability or mental deficiency at less than the minimum wage herein provided. Such permits shall combs, air-combs, blowers, razors, and eyebrow tweezers.

(C) A reasonable deposit may be required as security for the return of the items furnished by the employer under provisions of subsections (A) and (B) of this section upon issuance of a receipt to the employee for such deposit. Such deposits shall be made pursuant to Section 400 and following of the Labor Code. All items furnished by the employer shall be returned by the employee upon completion of the job.

10. MEALS AND LODGING

(A) "Meal" means an adequate, well-balanced serving of a variety of wholesome, nutritious foods.

"Lodging" means living accommodations which are adequate, decent, and sanitary according to usual and customary standards. Employees shall not be required to share a bed.

(B) When meals or lodging are furnished by the employer as part of the employee's compensation and when pursuant to a voluntary written agreement between the employer and the employee, such meals and lodging are to be credited towards the employer's minimum wage obligation, such meals and lodging may not be evaluated in excess of the following:

Room occupied alone		$12.00 per week
Room shared		$9.60 per week
Apartment—two-thirds (⅔) of the ordinary rental value, and in no event more than		$140.00 per month
Where a couple are both employed by the employer, two-thirds (⅔) of the ordinary rental value, and in no event more than		$210.00 per month
Meals:	Breakfast	$ .90
	Lunch	$1.25
	Dinner	$1.65

(C) Meals evaluated as part of the minimum wage must be bona fide meals consistent with the employee's work shift. Deductions shall not be made for meals not received nor lodging not used.

(D) If, as a condition of employment, the employee must live at the place of employment or occupy quarters owned or under the control of the employer, then the employer may not charge rent in excess of the values listed herein.

11. MEAL PERIODS

(A) No employer shall employ any person for a work period of more than five (5) hours without a meal period of not less than thirty (30) minutes, except that when a work period of not more than six (6) hours will complete the day's work the meal period may be waived by mutual consent of employer and employee. Unless the employee is relieved of all duty during a thirty (30) minute meal period, the meal period shall be considered an "on duty" meal period and counted as time worked. An "on duty" meal period shall be permitted only when the nature of the work prevents an employee from being relieved of all duty and when by written agreement between the parties an on-the-job paid meal period is agreed to.

(B) In all places of employment where employees are required to eat on the premises, a suitable place for that purpose shall be designated.

12. REST PERIODS

Every employer shall authorize and permit all employees to take rest periods, which insofar as practicable shall be in the middle of each work period. The authorized rest period time shall be based on the total hours worked daily at the rate of ten (10) minutes net rest time per four (4) hours or major fraction thereof.

However, a rest period need not be authorized for employees whose total daily work time is less than three and one-half (3½) hours. Authorized rest period time shall be counted as hours worked for which there shall be no deduction from wages.

OCCUPATIONAL SAFETY AND HEALTH STANDARDS

The Occupational Safety and Health Standards Board (Cal/OSHA) now regulates some matters formerly regulated by the Industrial Welfare Commission. For this reason, sections in previous Industrial Welfare Commission orders which referred to protective garments, drinking water and washing facilities, toilet rooms, first aid, floors, cleanliness and upkeep, lighting, ventilation, and exits do not appear in this Order.

Information on matters of occupational health and safety can be obtained from the Division of Industrial Safety, Department of Industrial Relations, State of California, at P.O. Box 603, San Francisco 94101, or from its district offices.

20. INSPECTION

The Commission and duly authorized representatives of the Division shall be allowed free access to any office or establishment covered by this Order to investigate and gather data regarding wages, hours, working conditions, and employment practices, and shall be permitted to inspect and make excerpts from any and all relevant records and to question all employees for such purposes.

The investigations and data gathering shall be conducted in a reasonable manner calculated to provide the necessary surveillance of employment practices and the enforcement of the Commission's orders.

21. PENALTIES

Failure, refusal, or neglect to comply with any of the provisions of this Order is a violation of the Labor Code of the State of California and is punishable by fine or imprisonment or both.

See excerpts from Labor Code, Sections 1196 and 1199.

22. SEPARABILITY

If the application of any provision of this Order, or any section, subsection, subdivision, sentence, clause, phrase, word, or portion of this Order should be held invalid or unconstitutional or unauthorized or prohibited by statute, the remaining provisions thereof shall not be affected thereby, but shall continue to be given full force and effect as if the part so held invalid or unconstitutional had not been included herein.

23. POSTING OF ORDER

Every employer shall keep a copy of this Order posted in an area frequented by employees where it may be easily read during the work day. Where the location of work or other conditions make this impractical, every employer shall keep a copy of this Order and make it available to every employee upon request.

. . . .

Order 5-68, enacted September 26, 1967 and amended February 20, 1968, and Order 1-74, enacted December 4, 1973, are hereby rescinded as and of the date when this Order becomes effective, October 18, 1976.

Dated at Sacramento, California, the twenty-seventh day of July, 1976.

INDUSTRIAL WELFARE COMMISSION
STATE OF CALIFORNIA
Howard Alan Carver, Chairperson
Joyce R. Valdez
Mike R. Elorduy
Jackie Walsh
Yvonne P. Aguilar

James L. Quillin, Chief
Division of Labor Standards Enforcement

Excerpts from Labor Code

SECTION 18. "Person" means any person, association, organization, partnership, business trust, or corporation.

SECTION 403. If cash is received as a bond it shall be deposited in a savings account in a bank authorized to do business in this State, and may be withdrawn only upon the joint signatures of the employer and the employee or applicant.

Cash put up as a bond shall be accompanied by an agreement in writing made by the employer and employee or applicant, setting forth the conditions under which the bond is given.

SECTION 1193.6. The department or division may, with the consent of the employee or employees affected, commence and prosecute a civil action to recover unpaid minimum wages or unpaid overtime compensation owing to any employee under the provisions of this chapter or the orders of the commission, and, in addition to such wages and compensation, shall be entitled to recover costs of suit. The consent of any employee to the bringing of any such action shall constitute a waiver on the part of the employee of his or her cause of action under Section 1194 unless such action is dismissed without prejudice by the department or the division.

SECTION 1196. Any employer who discharges, threatens to discharge, or in any other manner discriminates against any employee because the employee has testified or is about to testify, or because the employer believes that the employee will testify in any investigation or proceedings relative to the enforcement of this chapter, is guilty of a misdemeanor.

SECTION 1199. Every employer or other person acting either individually or as an officer, agent, or employee of another person is guilty of a misdemeanor and is punishable by a fine of not less than fifty dollars ($50) or by imprisonment for not less than 30 days, or by both, who does any of the following:

(a) Requires or causes any employee to work for longer hours than those fixed, or under conditions of labor prohibited by an order of the commission.

(b) Pays or causes to be paid an employee a wage less than the minimum fixed by an order of the commission.

(c) Violates or refuses or neglects to comply with any provision of this chapter or any order or ruling of the commission.

(d) Pays or causes to be paid any employee a wage less than the rate paid to an employee of the opposite sex as required by Section 1197.5 of this code.

(e) Reduces the wages of any employee in order to comply with Section 1197.5.

EMPLOYMENT OF MINORS: Persons under 18 are required to obtain work permits, and employers of minors under 16 are required to obtain permits to employ. Permits are obtained from school districts. Refer to Labor Code Sections 1285 to 1311 and 1390 to 1390 for restrictions on the employment of minors.

POST AND KEEP POSTED WHERE EMPLOYEES MAY READ

DISTRICT OF COLUMBIA MINIMUM WAGE AND INDUSTRIAL SAFETY BOARD

Wage Order No. 10

HOTEL, RESTAURANT, APARTMENT BUILDING, AND ALLIED OCCUPATIONS

Effective May 22, 1976

(This wage order supersedes Wage Order No. 10, effective June 13, 1972.)

TO WHOM IT MAY CONCERN—TAKE NOTICE.

Pursuant to the authority vested in it by Reorganization Order No. 38, as amended, and by Commissioners' Order No. 68-332, the Minimum Wage and Industrial Safety Board of the District of Columbia does hereby order that:

1. APPLICABILITY OF THIS WAGE ORDER.—This wage order applies to employees in the occupations defined in section 2(a) in the following industries (industry code designation of the "Standard Industrial Classification Manual, 1972" is indicated in parentheses): eating and drinking places (including eating and drinking places (including eating and drinking places (58); operators of apartment buildings (6513); operators of dwellings other than apartment buildings (6514); hotels, rooming houses, camps, and other lodging places (70).

2. DEFINITIONS.—As used in this wage order:

(a) **HOTEL, RESTAURANT, APARTMENT BUILDING, AND ALLIED OCCUPATIONS.**—The term "hotel, restaurant, apartment building, and allied occupations" includes:

(1) any business or part thereof engaged in providing lodging for hire including but not limited to apartment buildings, residential buildings, hotels, motels, clubs, camps, and other lodging places;

(2) any condominium or cooperative association operating, managing, or providing services to residents of a residential building; and

(3) any business or part thereof engaged in preparing and serving food or beverages or providing catering or carry-out and all activities connected with or incidental to the operation of such businesses or parts thereof, except beauty culture, laundry, and dry cleaning activities. Concessions are not covered by this wage order unless engaged in a business mentioned in subparagraphs (1), (2) or (3) of this paragraph.

(b) **ADULT LEARNER.**—The term "adult learner" means a person 18 years of age or over who has been employed in hotel, restaurant, apartment building, and allied occupations for a period not to exceed thirty calendar days regardless of the number of hours worked during such period.

(c) **ATTENDANT AT A PARKING LOT OR PARKING GARAGE.**—The term "attendant at a parking lot or parking garage" means any person who is employed to park or supervise the parking of automobiles at a parking lot or parking garage. A person employed as a cashier, guard, or maintenance man shall not be deemed an "attendant at a parking lot or parking garage."

(d) **EMPLOY.**—The term "employ" includes to suffer or permit to work.

(e) **EMPLOYEE.**—The term "employee" includes any individual employed by an employer in hotel, restaurant, apartment building, and allied occupations, except that such term shall not include:

(1) any individual who, without payment or expectation of any gain, directly or indirectly, volunteers to engage in the activities of an educational, charitable, religious, or nonprofit organization;

(2) any lay member elected or appointed to office within the discipline of any religious organization and engaged in religious functions; or

(3) any individual employed as a casual babysitter in or about the residence of the employer.

(f) **EMPLOYER.**—The term "employer" includes any individual, partnership, association, corporation, business trust, or any person or group of persons, acting directly or indirectly in the interest of an employer in relation to an employee, but shall not include the United States or the District of Columbia.

(g) **GRATUITIES.**—The term "gratuities" means voluntary monetary contributions received by an employee from a guest, patron, or customer for services rendered, except that the following shall not be deemed "gratuities": (1) compulsory service charges; (2) charges for banquet facilities for later distribution to employees; and (3) amounts required to be accounted for or turned over to the employer. An employer taking a gratuity allowance from the wage of an employee shall have the burden of proving the employee received in gratuities at least as much as the gratuity allowance taken.

(h) **HANDICAPPED WORKER.**—The term "handicapped worker" means a person whose earning capacity has been determined by the Minimum Wage and Industrial Safety Board to be impaired by physical or mental deficiency or injury for the work he is to perform.

(i) **REGULAR RATE.**—The term "regular rate" includes all remuneration for employment paid to, or on behalf of, the employee, but shall not be deemed to include the items set forth in the Fair Labor Standards Act of 1938, as amended, section 7(e)(1), (2), (3), (4), (5), (6), and (7). Extra compensation paid as described in section 7(e)(5), (6), and (7) shall be creditable toward overtime compensation payable pursuant to this wage order.

(j) **SERVICE EMPLOYEE.**—The term "service employee" means waiter (including counter-waiter), bus boy, bellman, hotel doorman, or hat checker.

(k) **SPLIT SHIFT.**—The term "split shift" means a schedule of daily hours in which the hours worked are not consecutive, except that a schedule including not more than one hour off for meals does not exceed one hour shall not be deemed a "split shift."

(l) **UNIFORM.**—The term "uniform" means any item of clothing (including hats and shoes) or ornament worn by the employee as a condition of employment. It shall be a presumption that uniforms are worn as a condition of employment if such clothing is of a similar pattern or color (including black and white), contains the employer's name or insignia, or forms part of the decorative pattern of the establishment.

(m) **WAGE.**—The term "wage" means compensation due to an employee by reason of his employment, payable in legal tender of the United States or checks on banks convertible into cash on demand at full face value, including such allowances as may be permitted by regulation issued under section 3, 6, 7, or 8 of the District of Columbia Minimum Wage Act of 1918, as amended.

(n) **WORKING TIME.**—The term "working time" means all time the employee is (1) required to be on the employer's premises, on duty, or at a prescribed place; (2) permitted to work; or (3) required to travel in connection with the business of the employer. Interpretations as to "constitutes" working time" shall be made in accordance with Title 29 Code of Federal Regulations, Part 785, Hours Worked Under the Fair Labor Standards Act of 1938, as amended, except that references to interpretations of the Portal-to-Portal Act shall have no force and effect.

(o) **WORKWEEK.**—The term "workweek" means a fixed and regularly recurring period of seven consecutive days.

3. MINIMUM WAGE.—No employer shall employ any employee at a wage less than **$2.80** for each hour of working time, except that an employer subject to the rent control provisions of the District of Columbia Rental Accommodations Act of 1975 shall pay a wage not less than **$2.50** an hour to any employee employed in a building in which rents are controlled, provided the employer is unable to pass on any wage increase required by this wage order.

(See sections 7, 8, 9, and 10 for minimum wages for employees who usually work 30 hours or less a week, employees under the age of 18, adult learners, and handicapped workers.)

4. OVERTIME COMPENSATION.—No employer shall employ any employee for workweek longer than forty hours unless such employee receives compensation for working time in excess of forty hours at a rate not less than one and one-half times the regular rate at which he is employed except that up to six hours of function time may be excluded from the computation of overtime compensation of an employee employed to work at functions for which the employee receives extra compensation and at which there is a prearranged service charge. Overtime compensation under the District of Columbia Minimum Wage Act of 1918, as amended, shall be paid in accordance with Title 29 Code of Federal Regulations, Part 778, Overtime Compensation Under the Fair Labor Standards Act of 1938, as amended, except that sub-part A (General Consideration), Subpart E (Exceptions From the Regular Rate Principles), Subpart G (Miscellaneous), and section 778.101 (Maximum Nonovertime Hours) shall have no force and effect.

5. EXEMPTIONS.—The minimum wage and overtime provisions of sections 3 and 4 shall not apply with respect to any employee employed in a bona fide executive, administrative, or professional capacity, or in the capacity of outside salesman (as such terms are defined by the Secretary of Labor under the Fair Labor Standards Act of 1938, as amended). The overtime provisions of section 4 shall not apply with respect to an attendant at a parking lot or parking garage.

6. EMPLOYEES COMPENSATED PRINCIPALLY BY COMMISSIONS.—No employer shall be deemed to have violated section 4 by employing any employee of a retail or service establishment in excess of 40 hours per workweek if (1) the regular

(g) **OVERTIME COMPENSATION.**

16. UNCONDITIONAL PAYMENT OF WAGES.—The employer shall unconditionally pay each employee the wages due the employee. Wages are not unconditionally paid if the employee pays directly or indirectly to the employer any part of the wages heretofore paid. This provision does not bar payroll deductions as authorized under this wage order or the District of Columbia Wage Payment and Wage Collection Law (D.C. Code, sections 36-601 through 36-610).

17. UNLAWFUL CHARGES.—The employer shall not charge an employee or require or permit an employee to pay directly or indirectly to the employer for breakage, walkouts, mistakes on customer checks, and similar charges.

rate of pay of such employee is in excess of one and one-half times the minimum hourly rate applicable to him under section 3, and (2) more than half his compensation for a representative period (not less than one month) represents commissions on goods or services. In determining the proportion of compensation representing commissions, all earnings resulting from the application of a bona fide commission rate shall be deemed commissions on goods or services without regard to whether the computed commissions exceed the draw or guarantee.

7. **PART-TIME RATE**—The employer shall pay an employee who usually works 30 hours or less a week a wage of $2.93 an hour, or a wage of $2.61 an hour if the employer is subject to the rent control provisions of the District of Columbia Rental Accommodations Act of 1975, provided the employer is unable to pass on any wage increase required by this wage order. This provision shall not apply to employees under the age of 18 or adult learners.

8. **EMPLOYEES UNDER THE AGE OF 18**—The employer may pay an employee under the age of 18 a wage of $2.25 an hour or $2.00 an hour if the employer is subject to the rent control provisions of the District of Columbia Rental Accommodations Act of 1975, provided the employer is unable to pass on any wage increase required by this wage order.

9. **ADULT LEARNERS**—The employer may pay an adult learner a wage of $2.50 an hour or $2.22 an hour if the employer is subject to the rent control provisions of the District of Columbia Rental Accommodations Act of 1975, provided the employer is unable to pass on any wage increase required by this wage order.

10. **HANDICAPPED WORKERS**—The Minimum Wage and Industrial Safety Board may issue a certificate to an employer authorizing the employment of the handicapped worker specified in the certificate at a wage less than the minimum wage prescribed in section 3 for such period of time and at such rate as shall be fixed in the certificate. The employer shall apply for a certificate before the employee begins work. Application shall be made in duplicate on forms provided by the Minimum Wage and Industrial Safety Board.

11. **MINIMUM DAILY WAGE**—The employer shall pay an employee for at least four hours for each day on which the employee reports for work under general or specific instructions but is given no work or is given less than four hours of work, except that if the employee is regularly scheduled for less than four hours a day, such employee shall be paid for the hours regularly scheduled. The minimum daily wage shall be calculated as follows: payment at the employee's regular rate for the hours worked plus payment at the applicable wage required by this wage order for the hours not worked as described above. This provision is not applicable to an employee who lives on the premises of the employer.

12. **SPLIT SHIFT AND EXCESSIVE SPREAD OF HOURS**—In addition to the wages required by this wage order, the employer shall pay the employee $2.80 or $2.50 if the employer is subject to the rent control provisions of the District of Columbia Rental Accommodations Act of 1975, provided the employer is unable to pass on any wage increase required by this wage order, for each day during which (1) the employee works a split shift or (2) the total time between the beginning and ending of the employee's workday exceeds ten hours. This provision is not applicable to an employee who lives on the premises of the employer.

13. **ITEMS OF EXPENSES INCURRED BY EMPLOYEE AS A CONDITION OF EMPLOYMENT**—

(a) **UNIFORMS AND PROTECTIVE CLOTHING**—In addition to the wages required by this wage order, the employer shall pay the cost of purchase, maintenance, and cleaning of (1) uniforms and special costumes and (2) protective clothing (including hats and shoes) required by the employer or by law, except that in lieu of purchasing, maintaining, and cleaning plain and washable uniforms and costumes, the employer may pay 7¢ per hour in addition to the wages required by this wage order. Such privilege of payment of 7¢ per hour shall not apply in the case of costumes or uniforms which are not plain and washable or in the case of protective clothing. When the employer purchases but the employee maintains and cleans plain and washable uniforms and costumes the payment shall be 5¢ per hour in addition to the wages required by this wage order; when the employer cleans and maintains but the employee purchases plain and washable uniforms and costumes the payment shall be 2¢ per hour in addition to the wages required by this wage order.

(b) **TOOLS AND TRAVEL EXPENSES**—In addition to the wages required by this wage order, the employer shall pay the cost of purchasing and maintaining tools and the cost of travel expenses incurred by the employee as a condition of employment.

14. **DEDUCTIONS**—No employer shall make any deductions, except those specifically authorized by law or court order or those allowances authorized in this wage order, which would bring the wages below those required by this wage order without the written consent of the employee and the written approval of the Minimum Wage and Industrial Safety Board.

15. **ALLOWANCES**—The following allowances may be made:

(a) **MEALS**—Not more than $1.10 for each meal furnished the employee by the employer with the following daily limitations: for four or less hours of work, an allowance for not more than one meal; for over four hours of work, an allowance for not more than two meals; for an employee who lives at the place of employment, an allowance for not more than three meals.

(b) **LODGING**—When the employer furnishes lodging to the employee, not more than three-fourths of the rental value of the lodging furnished as determined by a comparison with the value of similar accommodations in the vicinity of those furnished.

(c) **GRATUITY ALLOWANCE FOR SERVICE EMPLOYEES**—Not more than $1.45 an hour for gratuities for service employees as defined in this wage order. If the service employee receives less than $1.45 an hour in gratuities, the allowance shall not be more than such lesser amount.

18. **BASIS OF PAYMENT**—Irrespective of the basis of payment, whether time rate, piece rate, bonus, or commission, no employer shall pay any employee less than the wages required by this wage order.

19. **TIME OF PAYMENT**—Every employer shall establish a regular periodic pay day for each employee and shall pay to each employee on such pay day not less than the wages due for the pay period.

20. **RECORDS**—Every employer shall make, keep, and preserve for a period of not less than three years an accurate record for each employee containing the following information:

(a) Name in full, address, and occupation
(b) Date of birth if under 19 years of age
(c) Total number of hours worked each workday and each workweek
(d) If employee works a split shift, a daily record of the hours of beginning and stopping work and the hours of beginning and ending the meal recess
(e) Time of day and day of week on which employee's workweek begins
(f) Regular hourly rate of pay
(g) Basis on which wages are paid
(h) Total daily or weekly straight-time earnings and excess overtime earnings for the workweek, or, total earnings for nonovertime hours worked during the workweek and total earnings for overtime hours worked during the workweek
(i) For each pay period, deductions from and additions to wages
(j) Total gross and net wages paid each pay period
(k) Date of payment and the pay period covered by payment
(l) If employee is a service employee, the amount of gratuities reported by the employee as received per pay period or per month
(m) If employee is paid pursuant to section 6,
   (1) A symbol placed on the payroll record identifying each employee who is paid pursuant to section 6
   (2) An indication whether the employee's regular rate of pay in each workweek is in excess of one and one-half times the minimum hourly rate applicable to him under section 3 and that records are available to demonstrate this fact
   (3) A copy of the agreement or understanding under which section 6 is utilized or, if such agreement or understanding is not in writing, a summary of its terms including the basis of compensation and showing the applicable representative period and the date it was entered into and how long it remains in effect
   (4) Total compensation paid each pay period showing separately the amount of commissions and the amount of noncommission straight-time earnings.
(n) Evidence to support the employer's inability to pass on any wage increase required by this wage order due to the District of Columbia Rental Accommodations Act of 1975.

Such records shall be open and made available for inspection in the District of Columbia at any reasonable time by the Minimum Wage and Industrial Safety Board or any of its authorized representatives. An employer shall not be required to keep records specified in paragraphs (c), (d), (f), (g), (h), and (i) of this section for any employee employed in a bona fide executive, administrative, or professional capacity, or in the capacity of outside salesman (as such terms are defined by the Secretary of Labor under the Fair Labor Standards Act of 1938, as amended). An employer shall not be required to keep the records specified in paragraphs (f), (g), and (h) of this section for any employee employed pursuant to section 6.

21. **WAGE STATEMENT**—Every employer shall furnish to each employee at the time of payment of wages an itemized statement showing the date of the wage payment, gross wages paid (showing separately the earnings for overtime and nonovertime hours worked), an itemization of allowances and deductions from and additions to wages, net wages paid, hours worked during the pay period, and any other information as may be prescribed by the Minimum Wage and Industrial Safety Board, except that the wage statement need not be furnished to an employee employed in a bona fide executive, administrative, or professional capacity, or in the capacity of outside salesman (as such terms are defined by the Secretary of Labor under the Fair Labor Standards Act of 1938, as amended). For an employee employed pursuant to section 6, the itemized statement shall also show separately the amount of commissions and the amount of noncommission straight-time earnings.

22. **POSTING**—Every employer subject to this wage order shall keep a copy thereof posted in a conspicuous and accessible place in or about the premises wherein any employee covered by it is employed.

23. **COLLECTION OF UNPAID WAGES**—Any employer who fails to pay the wages required by this wage order shall pay to the Minimum Wage and Industrial Safety Board an amount equal to the unpaid wages, which amount shall be distributed by the Minimum Wage and Industrial Safety Board to employees due said unpaid wages. Unpaid wages which cannot be paid due to inability to locate employees or refusal of employees to accept said unpaid wages shall escheat to the District of Columbia government in accordance with D.C. Code, Sections 47-140-144.

24. **SEPARABILITY**—If any provision of this wage order, or the application thereof to any person or circumstances, is held invalid, the remainder of the wage order and the application thereof to other persons or circumstances shall not be affected thereby.

25. **REPEAL**—Wage Order No. 10 entitled "Hotel, Restaurant, and Allied Occupations," effective June 13, 1972, is hereby repealed, except with respect to rights accrued and liabilities incurred under said wage order prior to the effective date of this wage order and except with respect to violations of said wage order occurring prior to the effective date of this wage order.

26. **EFFECTIVE DATE**—This wage order becomes effective May 22, 1976.

BY ORDER OF THE DISTRICT OF COLUMBIA MINIMUM WAGE AND INDUSTRIAL SAFETY BOARD

SARAH H. NEWMAN, *Chairman*
JOSEPH A. BEAVERS
EDWARD L. FEGGANS

Attest: Richard R. Seideman, *Executive Secretary*
March 22, 1976

PENALTIES FOR VIOLATION—Any person who willfully violates any provision of this wage order shall upon conviction thereof be subject to a fine of not more than $10,000, or to imprisonment of not more than six months, or both. (See section 14 of the District of Columbia Minimum Wage Act of 1918, as amended.)

EMPLOYEE REMEDIES—(1) The employer is liable to the employee in the amount of any unpaid wages plus an equal amount as liquidated damages. (2) The Minimum Wage and Industrial Safety Board may take an assignment in trust of a wage claim for an employee and bring any legal action necessary to collect such claim. (3) The Minimum Wage and Industrial Safety Board may supervise the payment of unpaid wages owing employees. (See section 15 of the District of Columbia Minimum Wage Act of 1918, as amended.)

DISTRICT OF COLUMBIA MINIMUM WAGE AND INDUSTRIAL SAFETY BOARD
614 H Street, N.W., Room 615, Washington, D.C. 20001
629-3565

J-63978-76

Highlights of the

DISTRICT OF COLUMBIA WAGE-HOUR LAW

MINIMUM WAGE

INDUSTRY WAGE ORDERS

BEAUTY CULTURE INDUSTRY _____ **$2.50**

MANUFACTURING, WHOLESALE TRADE,
AND PRINTING AND PUBLISHING
INDUSTRIES ------------------------------------ **$2.46**

HOTEL, RESTAURANT, APARTMENT HOUSE,
AND ALLIED INDUSTRIES _____ **$2.80**
                                     (part time) **$2.93**

RETAIL TRADE INDUSTRY _____ **$2.25**

LAUNDRY AND DRY CLEANING
INDUSTRY -- **$2.40**

OVERTIME PAY

AFTER

40 HOURS PER WORKWEEK

NOT LESS THAN

1 1/2 TIMES THE EMPLOYEE'S
REGULAR RATE OF PAY

EXAMPLES OF
COMPUTING OVERTIME PAY

(Overtime pay must be computed on the basis of each workweek standing alone. Hours worked cannot be averaged over two or more workweeks. The regular rate is an hourly rate.)

IF PAY IS FIGURED AT AN HOURLY RATE

Employee is paid at a single hourly rate of $3.00, so that amount is his regular rate. For each overtime hour, he should receive $4.50 ($3.00 x 1½ = $4.50).

IF PAY IS BY SALARY

Employee is paid a salary for a specified number of hours a week. Divide the weekly salary ($160) by the specified hours (40) to secure his regular rate, $4.00 an hour. If he works more than 40 hours he would be entitled to $6.00 for each overtime hour ($4.00 x 1½ = $6.00), so that, if he worked 42 hours in one workweek, he should receive $12.00 ($6.00 x 2) for the two overtime hours, plus his salary of $160, or a total of $172. If this employee's salary is for a fixed number of hours in excess of 40 hours a week, he is due additional half-time at his regular rate for the number of fixed hours that are in excess of 40. Divide the weekly salary ($160) by the fixed hours (44) to secure his regular rate, $3.636 an hour. He is entitled to a weekly wage of $167.27, determined as follows: $160 + ((½ x $3.636) x 4). If he should work in excess of the fixed hours, he is due 1½ the regular rate for each hour in excess of 44.

Employee is paid a straight-time salary for whatever number of hours he works in a workweek. Divide the straight-time weekly salary ($176) by the number of hours he works in a week to secure his regular rate. His regular rate and overtime pay will vary from week to week. When he works 44 hours in one week his regular rate will be $4.00 an hour, and his additional overtime pay will be $2.00 an hour ($176 ÷ 44 = $4.00 and $4.00 ÷ 2 = $2.00). His total week's pay would be $184 ($176 + ($2.00 x 4) = $184). If he works 48 hours the next week, his regular rate will be $3.666 an hour, and his additional pay will be $1.833 an hour ($176 ÷ 48 = $3.666 and $3.666 ÷ 2 = $1.833). His total week's pay would be $190.66 ($176 + ($1.833 x 8) = $190.66).

> Employee paid on a salary basis who works more than 40 hours during a workweek must be paid overtime compensation in addition to salary.

Employee is paid twice a month for a 40-hour workweek. Convert the semimonthly salary ($260) into its weekly equivalent, $120 ($260 x 24 pay periods ÷

52 weeks = $120). His regular rate is $3.00 an hour ($120 ÷ 40 hours = $3.00). If he were to work 44 hours in a workweek he should be paid $18 for the four overtime hours ($3.00 x 1½ x 4 hours = $18), in addition to his salary.

IF PAY IS WHOLLY OR PARTLY BY COMMISSION

To figure the regular rate of pay of an employee who receives a commission computed on a weekly basis, add the commission payment to the employee's other earnings in the workweek and divide the total by the number of hours worked in the week. For example, an employee is paid an hourly rate of $3.00 and in addition receives a commission. In a particular workweek he worked 44 hours and received a commission of $6.60. His overtime and total pay would be computed as follows:

$3 x 44 hrs. + $6.60 comm. = $138.60 straight-time earnings

$138.60 ÷ 44 hrs. = $3.15 regular rate of pay

$3.15 x ½ = $1.575 half-time rate of pay

$1.575 x 4 overtime hrs. = $6.30 overtime pay due

$138.60 + $6.30 = $144.90 total wages due.

When a commission is computed and paid on other than a weekly basis, it must be apportioned back over the workweeks during which it was earned and the employee must then receive additional overtime pay for each week in which he worked overtime. Until this is done he may receive overtime compensation of not less than 1½ times his hourly rate, exclusive of the commission payment.

If it is not practicable to allocate the commission among the workweeks in proportion to the amount actually earned or reasonably presumed to be earned each week, some other reasonable or equitable method must be adopted. One method is to assume the employee earns an equal amount of commission in each hour that he worked during the period. Then, for example, if an employee received $19.20 in commissions for a period of 96 hours including 16 overtime hours (two workweeks of 48 hours each), the $19.20 would be divided by 96, giving a $0.20 increase in the hourly rate. The employee would be due an additional $0.10 for each of the 16 overtime hours, or $1.60.

STATE OF HAWAII

DEPARTMENT of LABOR and INDUSTRIAL RELATIONS

ENFORCEMENT DIVISION   888 MILILANI ST., HONOLULU 96813

NOTICE TO EMPLOYEES

Under the HAWAII WAGE and HOUR LAW

MINIMUM WAGE IS $2.40 * AN HOUR FROM JULY 1, 1975

OVERTIME AFTER 40 HOURS A WEEK

* Tips may be considered as wages under certain conditions.

The above minimum wage and maximum hour standards also apply to employment covered by the federal Fair Labor Standards Act whenever such standards are higher than those prescribed by the federal law.

The Hawaii Wage and Hour Law provides for specific exemptions from the minimum wage and/or overtime pay provisions for certain types of employment. This law also requires employers to maintain time records and provides various methods for the computation of overtime pay.

BACK WAGES MAY BE RECOVERED: An employee may bring suit against his employer to recover wages withheld or he may designate an agent or the Director of Labor and Industrial Relations to file suit in his behalf. Suits to recover such back wages must be filed within six years from the time the minimum wages and/or overtime pay became due.

WAGE DISCRIMINATION PROHIBITED: The law prohibits discrimination in any way in the payment of wages as between persons of different races or religion or as between sexes.

ENFORCEMENT: The State may bring civil or criminal action against employers who violate any provision of the Hawaii Wage and Hour Law.

YOU MAY OBTAIN MORE INFORMATION FROM THE OFFICES OF THE ENFORCEMENT DIVISION OF THE DEPARTMENT OF LABOR AND INDUSTRIAL RELATIONS LOCATED AT:

888 Mililani St. Honolulu	State Building Hilo	Ashihara Building Kealakekua	State Building Wailuku	State Building Lihue

(The posting of this notice in conspicuous places where employees subject to this law are employed is required by the Hawaii Wage and Hour Law.)

Director of Labor and Industrial Relations

STATE OF HAWAII

DEPARTMENT of LABOR and INDUSTRIAL RELATIONS
ENFORCEMENT DIVISION

NOTICE TO EMPLOYEES

UNDER THE PAYMENT OF WAGES AND OTHER COMPENSATION LAW YOUR EMPLOYER MUST:

- Pay all wages due you at least twice a month on regular paydays designated in advance, or once a month on regular pay-days designated in advance if the majority of your employer's employees so elect by secret ballot or if your employer is so authorized by the Director of Labor;

- Pay you within 7 days after the end of the pay period, or within 15 days if your employer is so authorized by the Director of labor;

- Pay you in cash or in checks convertible into cash on demand at full face value;

- Notify you in writing, at the time of hiring of your rate of pay, and of the day, hour, and place of payment of wages;

- Notify you in writing or through a posted notice of any changes on pay arrangements prior to the time of such changes, and also of his policies with regard to vacation pay and sick leave;

- Furnish you with pay statement at payday showing your gross wages, itemized deductions, net pay, date of payment and pay period covered by the payment;

- Pay to your spouse or adult child your earned wages including vacation and sick leave pay. Spouse must apply to employer within 30 days after your death.

YOUR EMPLOYER MAY DEDUCT FROM YOUR WAGES: State and federal withholding taxes; amounts specified by court orders; and amounts authorized by you in writing; but MAY NOT COLLECT, DEDUCT OR OBTAIN AUTHO-RIZATION TO DEDUCT FOR: (1) fines; (2) cash shortage in a common money till, cash box or register used by you and someone else; (3) breakage; (4) losses due to your acceptance of checks which are later dishonored if your employer has authorized you to accept checks; (5) losses due to faulty workmanship, lost or stolen property, damage to property, default of customer credit or non-payment for goods or services received by customer, unless such losses are due to your wilful or intentional disregard of your employer's interest; or (6) cost of required physical examination or medical report.

- The employer must pay for the loss of expected wages if you are terminated after giving a required advance notice of termination but prior to the last day as stated in said notice.

UNPAID WAGES MAY BE RECOVERED

- The Department of Labor is authorized to collect on your behalf your unpaid wages and to file civil suit, if necessary, at no cost to you. Claims must be filed within one year. Certain executives, administrators, supervisors, professionals, and outside salesmen are not provided our free collection service.

YOU MAY OBTAIN MORE INFORMATION FROM THE OFFICES OF THE ENFORCEMENT DIVISION OF THE DEPARTMENT OF LABOR AND INDUSTRIAL RELATIONS LOCATED AT:

888 Mililani St. Honolulu	State Building Hilo	Ashihara Building Kealakekua	State Building Wailuku	State Building Lihue

(Chapter 388, Hawaii Revised Statutes, requires the posting of the notice in a place accessible to employees.)

Joshua C. Agsalud

Director of Labor and Industrial Relations

(2/75)

illinois
department
of labor

NOTICE

to employer & employee

EMPLOYERS ARE REQUIRED TO POST THIS NOTICE IN A CONSPICUOUS PLACE FOR ALL EMPLOYEES.

THE DISPLAY OF THIS NOTICE FULFILLS ALL ILLINOIS DEPARTMENT OF LABOR POSTING REQUIREMENTS.*

WH1675
3-75

MICHIGAN MINIMUM WAGE LAW

INCLUDING

OVERTIME AND EQUAL PAY PROVISIONS

NOTE: NEW INCREASE IN MICHIGAN MINIMUM WAGE

Sec. 4. (1) The minimum hourly rate shall be:
(a) Beginning January 1, 1978, $2.65
(b) Beginning January 1, 1979, $2.90
(c) Beginning January 1, 1980, $3.10
(d) Beginning January 1, 1981, $3.25

ACT 154 of 1964

AN ACT to fix minimum wages for employees within this state; to prohibit wage discrimination; to provide for the administration and enforcement of this act; and to prescribe penalties for the violation of this act.

HISTORY: Am. 1971, p. 107, Act 62, Eff. Mar. 30, 1972.

The People of the State of Michigan enact:

408.381 Minimum wage law of 1964; short title. [M.S.A. 17.255(1)]
Sec. 1. This act shall be known and may be cited as the "minimum wage law of 1964".

408.382 Same; definitions. [M.S.A. 17.255(2)]
Sec. 2. As used in this act:
(a) "Commissioner" means the commissioner of labor.
(b) "Employee" means an individual between the ages of 18 and 65 years employed by an employer on the premises of the employer or at a fixed site designated by the employer, or a minor employed under section 23 of Act No. 157 of the Public Acts of 1947, being section 409.23 of the Michigan Compiled Laws.
(c) "Employer" means any person, firm or corporation, including the state and its political subdivisions; agencies and instrumentalities, and any person acting in the interest of such employer, who employs 4 or more employees at any one time within any calendar year. Such employer shall be subject to this act during the remainder of such calendar year.
(d) "Employ" means to engage, suffer or permit to work.

HISTORY: Am. 1966, p. 383, Act 269, Imd. Eff. July 12; — Am. 1974, p. , Act 304, Eff. Apr. 1, 1975

408.383 Prohibited Rate. [M.S.A. 17.255(3)]
Sec. 3. No employer shall pay any employee at a rate of less than prescribed in this act.

HISTORY: Am. 1966, p. 383, Act 269, Eff. Mar. 1, 1967.

408.384 Minimum hourly rates; changes in cost of living. [M.S.A. 17.255(4)]
Sec. 4. (1) The minimum hourly rate shall be:

(a) Beginning July 1, 1971, $1.60.
(b) Beginning April 1, 1975, $2.00.
(c) Beginning January 1, 1976, $2.20.
(d) Beginning January 1, 1977, $2.30.

(2) It is the intent of the legislature that any increases or decreases in the minimum hourly rate, established in this act after 1967, shall reflect corresponding increases or decreases in the cost of living.

HISTORY: Am. 1970, p. 91, Act 36, Imd. Eff. June 24; — Am. 1974, p. , Act 304, Eff. Apr. 1, 1975.

408.384a Compensation for overtime; exclusions. [M.S.A. 17.255(4a)]
Sec. 4a. (1) An employee shall receive compensation at not less than 1½ times the regular rate at which the employee is employed for employment in any workweek in excess of:

(a) 48 hours beginning April 1, 1975.
(b) 46 hours beginning May 1, 1975.
(c) 44 hours beginning May 1, 1976.
(d) 40 hours beginning May 1, 1977.

(2) Subsection (1) shall not apply to an employee:
(a) Who is not an employee as defined by the federal fair labor standards act of 1938, as amended, being 29 U.S.C. 201 to 219.
(b) Who is exempt from the maximum hours provisions of the federal fair labor standards act, pursuant to section 13 of that act, being 29 U.S.C. section 213, unless the employee is:
(i) An employee of a hotel, motel, or restaurant other than an employee of a hotel, motel, or restaurant who is exempt from the maximum hours provisions of the federal fair labor standards act, under section 13(A)(1) of that act, as amended, being 29 U.S.C. section 213.
(ii) An employee of a retail or service establishment other than an employee of a retail or service establishment who is exempt from the maximum hours provisions of the federal fair labor standards act, under section 13(A)(1) of that act, being 29 U.S.C. section 213.
(c) Who is subject to sections 7 (b) to 7 (n) of the federal fair labor standards act, being 29 U.S.C. sections 207 (b) to 207 (n).

HISTORY: Add. 1974, p. , Act 304, Eff. Apr. 1, 1975: Am. 1975, p. . Act 1975, Eff. Apr. 1, 1975.

408.385 Wage deviation board; appointment, officers, quorum, compensation, expenses. [M.S.A. 17.255(5)]
Sec. 5. After the effective date of this act, the governor shall appoint, with the advice and consent of the senate, a wage deviation board composed of 3 representatives of the employers, 3 representatives of the employees and 3 persons representing the public; 1 of the last 3 shall be designated as chairman. Members shall serve for terms of 3 years, except that of the members first appointed, 1 from each group shall be appointed for 1 year, 1 for 2 years and 1 for 3 years. The commissioner shall be secretary of the wage deviation board. A majority of the members of the board constitutes a quorum and the recommendation or report of the board requires a vote of not less than a majority of its members. Members of the board shall receive compensation of $25.00 per day for not more than 75 days per year, and the chairman $35.00 per day for not more than 150 days per year, and may be reimbursed for actual and necessary expense while on official duty.

HISTORY: Am. 1965, p. 433, Act 255, Imd. Eff. July 21; — Am. 1966, p. 217, Act 191, Eff. Mar. 10, 1967.

408.386 Rules. [M.S.A. 17.255(6)]
Sec. 6. The commissioner may promulgate rules necessary for administration of this act pursuant to Act No. 306 of the Public Acts of 1969, as amended, being sections 24.201 to 24.315 of the Michigan Compiled Laws.

HISTORY: Am. 1970, p. 91, Act 36, Imd. Eff. June 24; — Am. 1974, p. , Act 304, Eff. Apr. 1, 1975.

408.387 Wage deviation board; determination of deductions; apprentices, learners, handicapped persons. [M.S.A. 17.255(7)]
Sec. 7. On petition of a party in interest or on its own motion, the wage deviation board shall:
(a) Determine the amount of the gratuities and the value to the employee of board and lodging and apparel or other items or services customarily furnished to an employee for his benefit, and establish therefrom a reasonable deduction from the minimum wage set in this act to be paid by the employer. In no case shall the total deduction allowed be more than 25% of the hourly wage rate. The board may grant a stay of present employment situation until such determination.
(b) Establish a suitable scale of rates for apprentices, learners, physically and mentally handicapped persons who are clearly unable to meet normal production standards, which may be less than the regular minimum wage rate for experienced and nonhandicapped workers.

HISTORY: Am. 1966, p. 383, Act 269, Eff. Mar. 1, 1967.

408.387a Reduction of wages because of gratuities. [M.S.A. 17.255(7a)]
Sec. 7a. The wage of an employee shall not be reduced because the employee receives gratuities unless all of the following occur:
(a) The gratuities are proven gratuities as indicated by the employee's declaration for federal insurance contribution act purposes.
(b) The employee was informed by the employer of the provisions of this section.

HISTORY: Add 1974, p. , Act 304, Eff. Apr. 1, 1975.

408.388 Wage deviation board; data from employer, hearings. [M.S.A. 17.255(8)]
Sec. 8. The wage deviation board may request data of any employer, subject to the provisions of this act, as to the wages paid and hours worked by his employees and may hold such hearings as it deems necessary in obtaining this information.

408.389 Same; report, filing. [M.S.A. 17.255(9)]
Sec. 9. The wage deviation board shall submit its report to the commissioner who shall file it in his office as a public record together with the regulations established by the board.

408.390 Same; reconsideration of deviated wage rate. [M.S.A. 17.255(10)]
Sec. 10. At any time after a deviated wage rate has been in effect for 6 months or more, the wage deviation board may reconsider the rate.

408.391 Statement to employee, copy to commissioner; inspection; regulations and orders, posting. [M.S.A. 17.255(11)]
Sec. 11. Every employer, subject to the provisions of this act or of any regulation or order issued thereunder, shall furnish the employee a statement of the hours worked by the employee and of the wages paid to him listing deductions made each pay period and the employer shall furnish the commissioner upon demand a sworn statement of the same. Such records shall be open to inspection by the commissioner, his deputy or any authorized agent of the department at any reasonable time. Every employer subject to the provisions of this act or of any regulation or order issued under its provisions shall keep a copy of them posted in a conspicuous place in the area where employees are employed. The commissioner shall furnish copies of this act and the regulations and orders to employers without charge.

408.392 Enforcement of act; confidential character of information. [M.S.A. 17.255(12)]
Sec. 12. The commissioner of labor shall administer and enforce the provisions of this act; and at the request of the wage deviation board may investigate and ascertain the wages of employees of any employer subject to the provisions of this act. Members of the wage deviation board, the commissioner and his employees shall not reveal any facts or information obtained in the course of their duties, except insofar as they are required, pursuant to law, to report upon or take official action or testify in any proceedings regarding the affairs of any employer subject to this act.

408.393 Payment of less than a minimum wage; civil action for difference; violation of act, filing claim with commissioner; investigation. [M.S.A. 17.255(13)]
Sec. 13. If any employer pays any employee a lesser amount than the minimum wage provided in this act, the employee, at any time within 3 years, may (a) bring a civil action for the recovery of the difference between the amount paid and the minimum wage provided in this act and an equal additional amount as liquidated damages together with costs and such reasonable attorney's fees as may be allowed by the court, and/or (b) file a claim with the commissioner who shall investigate the claim. If the commissioner determines there is reasonable cause to believe that the employer has violated the provisions of this act and the commissioner is subsequently unable to obtain voluntary compliance by the employer within a reasonable period of time, the commissioner shall bring a civil action under the procedures and remedies as provided in clause (a). No contract or agreement between the employer and the employee or an acceptance of a lesser wage by the employee shall be a bar to the action.

HISTORY: Am. 1966, p. 383, Act 269, Imd. Eff. July 12.

408.394 Nonapplication of act; agricultural employers who contract on piecework basis; piece rate scale. [M.S.A. 17.255(14)]
Sec. 14. The provisions of this act shall not apply to any employer who is subject to the minimum wage provisions of the federal fair labor standards act of 1938, as amended, except in any case where application of such minimum wage provisions would result in a lower minimum wage than provided in this act, or to persons employed in summer camps for not more than 4 months, to handicapped employees covered by a blanket deviation certificate or other special certificate issued under sec. 14 (d) of the federal fair labor standards act of 1938, as amended, or to agricultural fruit growers, pickle growers and tomato growers, or other agricultural employers who traditionally contract for the harvesting on a piecework basis, as to those employees of such employers used for such harvesting until the board shall have acquired sufficient data to determine an adequate basis for the establishment of a scale of piecework and shall determine such a scale equivalent to the prevailing minimum wage for such employment, which determination shall occur no later than May 1, 1967. Such piece rate scale shall be equivalent to the minimum hourly wage in that when the payment by unit of production is applied to a worker of average ability and diligence in harvesting a particular commodity he shall receive an amount not less than the hourly minimum wage.

HISTORY: Am. 1965, p. 572, Act 296, Imd. Eff. July 22;—Am. 1966, p. 384, Act 269, Imd. Eff. July 12; Am. 1969, p. 325, Act 160, Imd. Eff. Aug. 5.

408.395 Discrimination against employees, penalty. [M.S.A. 17.255(15)]
Sec. 15. Any employer who discharges or in any other manner discriminates against any employee because the employee has served or is about to serve on the wage deviation board or has testified or is about to testify before the board, or because the employer believes that the employee may serve on the board or may testify before the board or in any investigation under the provisions of this act, and any person who violates any provision of this act or of any regulation or order issued under this act, is guilty of a misdemeanor.

408.396 Consistent discharge of employees, presumption. [M.S.A. 17.255(16)]
Sec. 16. Any employer who consistently discharges employees within 10 weeks of their employment and replaces the discharged employees without work stoppage is presumed to have discharged them to evade payment of the wage rates established in this act and shall be guilty of a misdemeanor.

HISTORY: Am. 1966, p. 384, Act 269, Eff. Mar. 1, 1967.

408.397 Minimum wage; discrimination based on sex. [M.S.A. 17.255(17)]
Sec. 17. (1) An employer having employees subject to the provisions of this act shall not discriminate between employees within an establishment on the basis of sex by paying wages to employees in the establishment at a rate less than the rate at which he pays wages to employees of the opposite sex in the establishment for equal work on jobs, the performance of which requires equal skill, effort and responsibility and which are performed under similar working conditions, except where the payment is made pursuant to (a) a seniority system; (b) a merit system; (c) a system which measures earnings by quantity or quality of production; (d) a differential based on a factor other than sex.
(2) An employer who is paying a wage differential in violation of this section shall not reduce the wage rate of an employee in order to comply with the provisions of this section.
(3) For purposes of administration and enforcement, any amounts owing to an employee which have been withheld in violation of this section shall be deemed to be unpaid minimum wages under this act.

HISTORY: Add. 1971, p. 107, Act 62, Eff. Mar. 30, 1972.

DEPARTMENT OF LABOR
Bureau of Safety and Regulation
Wage Hour Division
Lansing, Michigan
48926

TO BE POSTED IN A CONSPICUOUS PLACE

MINNESOTA FAIR LABOR STANDARDS ACT AND LABOR STANDARDS REGULATIONS

EFFECTIVE OCTOBER 1, 1976

The reason for the Minnesota Fair Labor Standards Act is to establish minimum wage and overtime compensation standards at levels that are adequate to maintain workers' health, efficiency and well being and to sustain their purchasing power and also to increase employment opportunities.

MINIMUM WAGE

$2.10 per hour if 18 years of age or older

$1.89 per hour if under 18 years of age

OVERTIME PAY

AFTER 48 HOURS A WEEK AT NOT LESS THAN
ONE AND A HALF TIMES THE EMPLOYEE'S REGULAR RA

PERSONS EXEMPT FROM COVER

The following persons are not covered by the provisio

1. Agricultural worker on a farm that has less than 2 weeks of employment or on a farm that has o
2. Farm-worker who is under 18 years of age.
3. Counselor in an organized resident or day c
4. Bona fide executive, administrative, or prof
5. Salesman who conducts no more than 20
6. Volunteer worker for a nonprofit organiza
7. Elected government official, member of go teer worker.
8. Police or fire department employee for a
9. Taxicab driver.
10. Individual babysitter.
11. Part-time worker in a carnival, circus, or fai
12. Part-time worker under 18 years of age wo
13. Conservation Officer (Nat. Resource Mgrs.
14. Individuals subject to qualifications and maxi tation.

OVERTIME EXCEPTIONS

1. Person paid on a commission or incentive basis tomobiles, trailers, trucks, or farm implements in overtime provision.
2. Worker in a health care facility (if agreed to before h period if he receives time-and-a-half compensation afte period.
3. Employee of the state or other political subdivision — time off monetary compensation.
4. Employee of a retail or service establishment whose regular rate of p times the applicable minimum wage rate and who receives more than hal commissions on goods or services — no overtime coverage.

OTHER PROVISIONS

A. MINIMUM WAGE RATE FOR MINORS: Employers claiming an employee is under 18 must have tificate included in the payroll records kept for such an employee. The age must be substan- birth certificate or an age certificate issued by the Department of Labor and Industry by the high school, may be paid not less than $1.89 an hour for the rolled in state approved high school vocational on-the-job programs, in Superintendent of Schools).

may be credited toward the minimum wage for meals and vided by the employer. The allowances are established for lodging. No employee is required to accept meals portion of a variety of wholesome, nutritious foods. owance credited, meals must be consistent with an plied by the employee, or no credit may be taken.

CREDIT: A credit for tip up to 25% of the applicable minimum wage rate, be credited toward the mi ice person who receives at least $20 per month in tips. A service ion performs the main services for a customer eds a consi nsate who benefit because the recipient shares to tip w toward their minimum wage. No employer may supply o nt records a statement for each pay period that the employee received an amount in tips oyer. The employer's records must also show in tips.

be made for shortages in money receipts or s, or for breakages.

worked which includes training time, call time, the employee must be either on the premises of in connection with his employment. In calculati- gular rate of pay is determined by dividing an vious credits granted) by the total hours worked. yee's pay for purposes of this calculation, and they ts for overtime work or work on scheduled days off; payments for occasional periods when no work is rofit-sharing plan or trust or bona fide thrift or savings ter than the second payday after they are earned.

PT BY THE EMPLOYER FOR A PERIOD OF THREE

E:
paid each pay period
s worked each day and each workweek,
including beginning and ending hours each day,
with A.M. and P.M. designations

Additional records may be required for special situations (see A, D, E).

For further information, write to
Department of Labor and Industry
Labor Standards Division
444 Lafayette Road
St. Paul, Minnesota 55101

This poster contains only a summary.
A copy of the complete law and
regulations is available, for a small fee, from

Documents Section
140 Centennial Building
St. Paul, MN 55155

PENALTIES

Any employer who pays an employee less than the wages and overtime compensation provided for by the Act shall be liable to the employee for (1) the full amount of such wages and overtime compensation (less any amount actually paid to the employee by the employer), (2) an additional equal amount, as liquidated damages, and (3) costs and such reasonable attorney's fees as may be allowed by a court. The Act prohibits employers from discharging or in any manner discriminating against an employee because of a complaint about wages to the employer or to the Department of Labor and Industry. Convictions under this section may result in a fine of not less than $500 nor more than $1000.

THIS SUMMARY MUST BE POSTED IN A CONSPICUOUS PLACE

SUMMARY OF MINIMUM WAGE ORDER FOR THE HOTEL INDUSTRY EFFECTIVE JANUARY 1, 1975

1. BASIC HOURLY RATE—ALL HOTELS
On and after January 1, 1975—$2.10 an hour
On and after January 1, 1976—$2.30 an hour

2. OVERTIME HOURLY RATE—ALL HOTELS
1½ times the basic hourly rate, before allowances for meals and lodging, but after allowances, if any, for tips.
over 40 hours a week for non-residential employees;
over 44 hours a week for residential employees.
Overtime must also be paid in resort hotels for hours worked on the seventh consecutive day in any week.

3. PART TIME HOURLY RATE
All-year hotels only for non-residential employees. Applies to part time work of 30 hours or less in a week.
On and after January 1, 1975—$2.15 an hour
On and after January 1, 1976—$2.35 an hour

4. YOUTH RATE—ALL HOTELS
An employer may apply for a certificate to pay youth under 18 years of age a minimum wage which is:
Effective 1/1/75—30¢ per hour
Effective 1/1/76—35¢ per hour
less than the applicable minimum wage. No more than 2 employees on any day or more than 10% of the total employees, whichever is greater, may be paid at the youth rate.

5. STUDENT RATE—RESORT HOTELS
Employers operating resort hotels may apply for a certificate to employ students as service employees at less than the above rates.

6. CALL-IN PAY—ALL HOTELS
Whenever a non-residential employee reports for work, the employer shall pay for at least: 3 hours for one shift of 3 consecutive hours or less; 6 hours for two shifts totalling 6 hours or less; 8 hours for three shifts totalling 8 hours or less.
This provision shall not apply to one employee in the establishment, and to students attending a full-time school on any day during the regular school year.

7. ADDITIONAL RATE FOR SPREAD OF HOURS—All-year hotels only
A non-residential employee shall receive an additional one hour's pay at the basic hourly rate before allowances for any day in which the spread of hours exceeds 10.

8. UNIFORMS—ALL HOTELS
If the employer fails to launder required uniforms, he shall pay an additional amount per week, as follows:

	Eff. 1/1/75 Per Week	Eff. 1/1/76 Per Week
If employee works:		
more than 30 hours	$2.65	$2.90
more than 20 hours to 30 hours	$2.00	$2.20
20 hours or less weekly	$1.30	$1.40

The employer shall reimburse an employee who purchases a required uniform.

9. TIP ALLOWANCE
ALL-YEAR HOTELS
On and after January 1, 1975:
45¢ per hour—if tips average 45¢ to 65¢ an hour.
65¢ per hour—if tips average 65¢ or more an hour

On and after January 1, 1976:
50¢ per hour—if tips average 50¢ to 70¢ an hour
70¢ per hour—if tips average 70¢ or more an hour

RESORT HOTELS
On and after January 1, 1975:
Service Employees:
45¢ per hour—if tips average 45¢ to 65¢ an hour
65¢ per hour—if tips average 65¢ to $1.50 an hour
75¢ per hour—if tips average more than $1.50 an hour

Chambermaids:
30¢ per hour—if tips average 30¢ to $1.50 an hour
50¢ per hour—if tips average more than $1.50 an hour

On and after January 1, 1976:
Service Employees:
50¢ per hour—if tips average 50¢ to 70¢ an hour
70¢ per hour—if tips average 70¢ to $1.50 an hour
85¢ per hour—if tips average more than $1.50 an hour

Chambermaids:
35¢ per hour—if tips average 35¢ to $1.50 an hour
55¢ per hour—if tips average more than $1.50 an hour

10. ALLOWANCES FOR MEALS AND LODGING
ALL-YEAR HOTELS
On and after January 1, 1975
Meals—75¢ per meal
Lodging—15¢ per hour
On and after January 1, 1976
Meals—80¢ per meal
Lodging—15¢ per hour

RESORT HOTELS
On and after January 1, 1975
Lodging and 3 meals—$4.15 per workday
Meals, no lodging—75¢ per meal
Lodging, no meals—15¢ per hour
On and after January 1, 1976
Lodging and 3 meals—$4.55 per workday
Meals, no lodging—80¢ per meal
Lodging, no meals—15¢ per hour

11. WAGE STATEMENTS AND RECORDS
Employers must provide each employee with a wage statement with every payment of wages showing hours worked, rates paid, gross wages, deductions and allowances, and net wages.
Employers must maintain for six years, and furnish for examination on the premises where employees work, a true record of daily and weekly hours of work, weekly wages, allowances and deductions.

12. OTHER WAGE ORDER PROVISIONS
The minimum wage order for the Hotel Industry contains a definition of the industry and other provisions including regulations relating to handicapped worker's certificate, basis of wage payment, deductions and expenses, and employment covered by more than one wage order.

13. EMPLOYEES COVERED BY FEDERAL LAW
Employees covered under the Federal Fair Labor Standards Act must be paid in accordance with the provisions of this wage order and also in accordance with higher Federal requirements, where applicable.

SUMMARY OF OTHER LABOR LAW PROVISIONS

1. PAYMENT OF WAGES
Manual workers must be paid weekly not later than 7 days after the end of the week in which wages are earned. Commission salesmen must be paid at least monthly and clerical and other workers at least semi-monthly.
All workers must be paid in cash unless a permit to pay by check is obtained from the Labor Department. Executive, administrative, and professional employees earning in excess of $200 a week are exempted from this requirement.

2. UNPAID WAGES AND FRINGE BENEFITS
If you have not been paid the minimum wage or have a claim for unpaid wages or if your employer has not provided wage supplements he has agreed to provide, the Labor Department will help you collect such wages or fringe benefits. Wage supplements include but are not limited to reimbursement for expenses; health, welfare and retirement benefits; and vacation, separation, or holiday pay.

3. ILLEGAL DEDUCTIONS OR CHARGES
No deductions may be made from wages except deductions authorized by law, or which are authorized in writing by the employee and are for his benefit. Authorized deductions include payments for insurance premiums, pension, contribution to charitable organizations, payments for U.S. bonds, union dues, and similar payments for the benefit of the employee.
An employer may not make any charge against wages, or require an employee to make any payment by separate transaction unless such charge or payment is permitted as a deduction from wages. Examples of illegal deductions or charges include payments by the employee for spoilage, breakage, cash shortages or losses, and cost and maintenance of required uniforms.

4. EQUAL PAY
A differential in rate of pay because of sex is prohibited.

5. ILLEGAL TIP APPROPRIATION
It is unlawful for your employer, or any other person, to demand or accept or retain any part of your tip earnings, including charges purported to be gratuities. However, practices in connection with hat-checking, banquets where a fixed percentage of a patron's bill is added for gratuities which are distributed to service employees, or the sharing of tips by a waiter with a busboy or similar employee are permitted.

6. HOURS AND DAY OF REST
*Every employee must be given 24 consecutive hours of rest weekly.
*Minors under 18 but over 16 may not be employed over 48 hours or 6 days weekly, nor between midnight and 6 a.m.
There are further restrictions for persons under 16 years of age, and for those under 17 years on school days.
*Schedules of hours of work for employees under 18 years of age and a day of rest schedule for all employees over 18 years who work on Sunday must be posted in the establishment.

*These provisions do not apply to resort or seasonal hotels in rural communities and in cities or villages with less than 15,000 population.

7. MEAL PERIODS
At least 45 minutes must be allowed for the noonday meal. Persons working more than 6 hours starting between 1 p.m. and 6 a.m. must be allowed at least 45 minutes midway within the work shift. Persons starting work before noon and continuing after 7 p.m. must also be allowed at least 20 minutes between 5 p.m. and 7 p.m. The Department of Labor may grant permission for shorter meal periods than as stated above.

8. CHILD LABOR
An employment certificate is required for any person under 18 years of age. No child under 14 years may be employed.

9. UNEMPLOYMENT INSURANCE
If you lose your job, get a "Record of Employment" slip from your employer and go to your nearest Unemployment Insurance office for help in finding a job and getting unemployment insurance payments.

10. WORKMEN'S COMPENSATION
If you are hurt on the job, notify your foreman or supervisor promptly and file a claim with the nearest office of the Workmen's Compensation Board. Board offices are located in New York City, Albany, Binghamton, Buffalo, Hempstead, Rochester, and Syracuse. Write or telephone any of these offices if you need claim forms or additional information.

11. DISABILITY BENEFITS
If you cannot work because of illness or injury incurred off the job, you may be entitled to payments under the Disability Benefits Law. File a Disability Benefits claim form with your employer or his insurance company. If you need claim forms or further information, write or telephone any office of the Workmen's Compensation Board. These are located in New York City, Albany, Binghamton, Buffalo, Hempstead, Rochester, and Syracuse.

12. HEALTH AND SAFETY
State regulations to protect workers against accidents on the job require safeguards against dangerous machinery and equipment, and environmental hazards such as poisonous fumes and substances, and against other unhealthful and dangerous conditions at work. Employers must follow these safety regulations.

13. PENALTIES
Any person who violates any provision of the Labor Law, or any rule, regulation or order issued thereunder is guilty of a misdemeanor, punishable by fine or imprisonment as provided by law.

FOR
LABOR
DEPARTMENT
USE
ONLY

Address inquiries, complaints or requests for additional copies of this poster to one of the offices of the Department of Labor listed below:

ALBANY 12201 State Office Bldg. Campus	BUFFALO 14202 65 Court St.	HEMPSTEAD 11550 175 Fulton Ave.	ROCHESTER 14614 155 Main St. W.	UTICA 13501 207 Genesee St.
BINGHAMTON 13901 44 Hawley St.	HAUPPAUGE 11787 Veterans Highway	NEW YORK CITY Two World Trade Center 10047 (main office) 163 West 125th St. 10027 (branch)	SYRACUSE 13202 333 East Washington St.	WHITE PLAINS 10603 30 Glenn St.

IR-106 (12-74) HOTEL   **POST CONSPICUOUSLY WHERE EMPLOYEES MAY READ**

STATE OF NEW YORK – DEPARTMENT OF LABOR
Labor Law Information Relating to Employment
IN THE RESTAURANT INDUSTRY

SUMMARY OF MINIMUM WAGE ORDER FOR THE RESTAURANT INDUSTRY, EFFECTIVE JANUARY 1, 1975

1. BASIC HOURLY RATE
On and after January 1, 1975 - $2.10 an hour
On and after January 1, 1976 - $2.30 an hour

2. PART-TIME HOURLY RATE
Applies to working time of 30 hours or less a week.
On and after January 1, 1975 - $2.15 an hour
On and after January 1, 1976 - $2.35 an hour

3. TIP ALLOWANCE FOR SERVICE EMPLOYEES
On and after January 1, 1975:
45¢ per hour—if tips average 45¢ to 65¢ an hour
65¢ per hour—if tips average 65¢ or more an hour
On and after January 1, 1976:
50¢ per hour—if tips average 50¢ to 70¢ an hour
70¢ per hour—if tips average 70¢ or more an hour
A service employee is an employee who receives at least 45¢ an hour in tips beginning January 1, 1975 and 50¢ an hour in tips beginning January 1, 1976.

4. OVERTIME
One and one half times the basic hourly rate, after allowance, if any, for tips, for working time over 40 hours in a week.

5. CALL-IN PAY
An employee who, by request or permission of the employer, reports for duty on any day shall be paid for at least
3 hours for one shift of 3 consecutive hours or less;
6 hours for two shifts totaling 6 hours or less;
8 hours for three shifts totaling 8 hours or less.
This provision does not apply to:
a. One employee in the establishment; and
b. Students attending a full-time school, on any day during the regular school year.

6. ADDITIONAL RATE FOR SPREAD OF HOURS
An employee shall receive an additional one hour's pay at the basic hourly rate before allowances, for each day in which spread of hours exceeds 10.

On and after January 1, 1975 $2.10 a day
On and after January 1, 1976 $2.30 a day

7. UNIFORMS
If the employer fails to launder required uniforms, he shall pay an additional amount per week, as follows:

	Eff. 1/1/75 Per Week	Eff. 1/1/76 Per Week
If employee works:		
more than 30 hours	$2.65	$2.90
more than 20 hours to 30 hours	$2.00	$2.20
20 hours or less weekly	$1.30	$1.40

The employer shall reimburse an employee who purchases a required uniform.

8. YOUTH RATE
An employer may apply for a certificate to pay youth under 18 years of age a minimum wage which is:
Effective 1/1/75 30¢ per hour
Effective 1/1/76 35¢ per hour
less than the applicable minimum wage specified in this order with certain limitations. No more than two employees on any day or more than 10 percent of the total employees, whichever is greater, may be paid at the youth rate.

9. ALLOWANCE FOR MEALS
On and after January 1, 1975 - 75¢ per meal
On and after January 1, 1976 - 80¢ per meal

10. ALLOWANCE FOR LODGING
On and after January 1, 1975
55¢ per day; $3.30 per week.
On and after January 1, 1976
60¢ per day; $3.60 per week.

11. WAGE STATEMENTS AND RECORDS
Employers must provide each employee with a wage statement with every payment of wages showing hours worked, rates paid, gross wages, deductions and allowances, and net wages.
Employers must maintain for six years, and furnish for examination on the premises where employees work, a true record of daily and weekly hours of work, weekly wages, allowances and deductions.

12. OTHER WAGE ORDER PROVISIONS
The minimum wage order for the Restaurant Industry contains a definition of the industry and other provisions including regulations relating to handicapped worker's certificate, basis of wage payment, deductions and expenses, and employment covered by more than one wage order.

13. EMPLOYEES COVERED BY FEDERAL LAW
Employees covered under the Federal Fair Labor Standards Act must be paid in accordance with the provisions of this wage order and also in accordance with higher Federal requirements, where applicable.

SUMMARY OF OTHER LABOR LAW PROVISIONS

1. PAYMENT OF WAGES
Manual workers must be paid weekly not later than 7 days after the end of the week in which wages are earned. Commission salesmen must be paid at least monthly and clerical and other workers at least semi-monthly.
All workers must be paid in cash unless a permit to pay by check is obtained from the Labor Department. Executive, administrative, and professional employees earning in excess of $200 a week are exempted from this requirement.

2. UNPAID WAGES AND FRINGE BENEFITS
If you have not been paid the minimum wage or have a claim for unpaid wages or if your employer has not provided wage supplements he has agreed to provide, the Labor Department will help you collect such wages or fringe benefits. Wage supplements include but are not limited to reimbursement for expenses; health, welfare and retirement benefits; and vacation, separation, or holiday pay.

3. ILLEGAL DEDUCTIONS OR CHARGES
No deductions may be made from wages except deductions authorized by law, or which are authorized in writing by the employee and are for his benefit. Authorized deductions include payments for insurance premiums, payments for U.S. bonds, union dues, and similar payments for the benefit of the employee.
An employer may not make any charge against wages, or require an employee to make any payment by separate transaction unless such charge or payment is permitted as a deduction from wages. Examples of illegal deductions or charges include payments by the employee for spoilage, breakage, cash shortages or losses, and cost and maintenance of required uniforms.

4. ILLEGAL TIP APPROPRIATION
It is unlawful, for your employer, or any other person, to de-
mand or accept or retain part of your tip earnings, including charges purported to be gratuities. However, practices in connection with hat-checking, banquets where a fixed percentage of a patron's bill is added for gratuities which are distributed to service employees, or the sharing of tips by a waiter with a busboy or similar employee are permitted.

5. EQUAL PAY
A differential in rate of pay because of sex is prohibited.

6. HOURS AND DAY OF REST
*Every employee must be given 24 consecutive hours of rest weekly.
*Minors under 18 but over 16 may not be employed over 48 hours or 6 days weekly, nor between midnight and 6 a.m.
There are further restrictions for persons under 16 years of age, and for those under 17 years of age on school days.
*Schedules of hours of work for employees under 18 years of age and a day of rest schedule for all employees over 18 years who work on Sunday must be posted in the establishment.
*These provisions do not apply to resort or seasonal restaurants in rural communities and in cities or villages with less than 15,000 population.

7. MEAL PERIODS
At least 45 minutes must be allowed for the noonday meal. Persons working more than 6 hours starting between 1 p.m. and 6 a.m. must be allowed at least 45 minutes midway within the work shift. Persons starting work before noon and continuing after 7 p.m. must also be allowed at least 20 minutes between 5 p.m. and 7 p.m. The Department of Labor may grant permission for shorter meal periods than as stated above.

8. CHILD LABOR
An employment certificate is required for any person under 18 years of age. No child under 14 years of age may be employed.

9. UNEMPLOYMENT INSURANCE
If you lose your job, get a "Record of Employment" slip from your employer and go to your nearest Unemployment Insurance office for help in finding a job and getting unemployment insurance payments.

10. WORKMEN'S COMPENSATION
If you are hurt on the job, notify your foreman or supervisor promptly and file a claim with the nearest office of the Workmen's Compensation Board. Board offices are located in New York City, Albany, Binghamton, Buffalo, Hempstead, Rochester, and Syracuse. Write or telephone any of these offices if you need claim forms or additional information.

11. DISABILITY BENEFITS
If you cannot work because of illness or injury incurred off the job, you may be entitled to payments under the Disability Benefits Law. File a Disability Benefits claim form with your employer or his insurance company. If you need claim forms or further information, write or telephone any office of the Workmen's Compensation Board. These are located in New York City, Albany, Binghamton, Buffalo, Hempstead, Rochester, and Syracuse.

12. HEALTH AND SAFETY
State regulations to protect workers against accidents on the job require safeguards against dangerous machinery and equipment, and environmental hazards such as poisonous fumes and substances, and against other unhealthful and dangerous conditions at work. Employers must follow these safety regulations.

13. PENALTIES
Any person who violates any provision of the Labor Law, or any rule, regulation or order issued thereunder is guilty of a misdemeanor, punishable by fine or imprisonment as provided by law.

FOR LABOR DEPARTMENT USE ONLY

Address inquiries, complaints or requests for additional copies of this poster to one of the offices of the Department of Labor listed below:

ALBANY 12201 — State Office Bldg. Campus
BUFFALO 14202 — 65 Court St.
HEMPSTEAD 11550 — 175 Fulton Ave.
ROCHESTER 14614 — 155 Main St. W.
UTICA 13501 — 207 Genesee St.
BINGHAMTON 13901 — 44 Hawley St.
HAUPPAUGE 11787 — Veterans Highway
NEW YORK CITY — Two World Trade Center 10047 (main office) 163 West 125th St. 10027 (branch)
SYRACUSE 13202 — 333 East Washington St.
WHITE PLAINS 10603 — 30 Glenn St.

IR-105 (12-74) Restaurant

POST CONSPICUOUSLY WHERE EMPLOYEES MAY READ

NORTH CAROLINA LABOR LAWS

(Abstracted from the General Statutes of North Carolina)

CHILD LABOR LAW

EMPLOYMENT CERTIFICATES. Minors under age 18 must obtain employment certificates from their county Director of Social Services. The minor must surrender the employment certificate to the employer upon the first day of work. The employer must keep the certificate on file as long as the minor is employed. Upon termination of the employment, the employer must immediately return the certificate to the minor, who then may take the certificate on to his or next job. These requirements do not apply to domestic and farm work. (G.S. 110-1 and 110-9)

PROHIBITED EMPLOYMENT.
* Minors under 18 may not work in, about, or in connection with any establishment where alcoholic liquors, including wine and beer, are manufactured, distributed, or sold, except in establishments holding "off premises" licenses only. One exception to this is that minors 16 or older may work in Grade A restaurants holding State ABC Board permits, but may not serve or dispense alcoholic beverages. (G.S. 110-7)
* Minors under 18 may not work in occupations designated hazardous by law. (G.S. 110-6 and 110-7)
* Minors under 16 may not work at manufacturing or mechanical establishments. (G.S. 110-1 and 110-6)
* Minors under 14 may not work in, about or in connection with any gainful occupation, except that minors age 12 or over may sell and deliver newspapers and magazines for not more than 10 hours per week. (G.S. 110-1 and 110-8)

HOURS OF WORK.
* For minors aged 16 and 17: 9 hours per day, 48 hours per week, 6 days per week, any time between 6 a.m. and 12 midnight.
* For minors aged 14 and 15: 8 hours per day, 40 hours per week, 6 days per week, any time between 7 a.m. and 7 p.m., but only 5 hours continuously without a 30-minute lunch period. On days when school is not in session, this age minor may work until 9 p.m. Combined hours of work and hours in school must not exceed 8 in any one day. (G.S. 110-2 and 110-3)

PENALTY FOR VIOLATION of any of the above sections or any of the child labor regulations is a fine of not less than $5 nor more than $50, or imprisonment for not more than 30 days, or both. (G.S. 110-20)

MAXIMUM HOUR LAW

WORKING HOURS. Maximum working hours for covered adult employees (age 18 or over) are 10 hours per day, 56 hours per week, and 12 days in any period of 14 consecutive days. (G.S. 95-17)

EXCEPTIONS. None of the above restrictions on working hours apply to:
* Employees whose employment is covered by, or in compliance with, the Fair Labor Standards Act (Federal Wage and Hour Law).
* Establishments employing fewer than four employees.
* Employment in agriculture, domestic service, cotton gins, bona fide office, foremanship, clerical, or supervisory jobs, executive positions, learned professions, commercial fishing, seasonal hotels and club houses, charitable institutions, hospitals, common carriers, public utilities, public employees, outside salespersons on commission basis. (G.S. 95-17)

SPREAD OF WORKING HOURS. Where the day is divided into two or more work periods for the same employee, all such periods shall be within 12 consecutive hours, except that in public eating places such periods shall be within 14 hours. (G.S. 95-17)

OVERTIME PAY. Any covered employee working more than 50 hours in any one week must be paid time and a half his or her regular rate of pay for such excess hours. (G.S. 95-17.1)

TIME RECORDS. Every employer must keep a timebook or record stating the name and occupation of each employee, the number of hours worked by him or her each day, and the amount of wages paid each pay period to each employee. (G.S. 95-20 and 110-5)

PENALTY FOR VIOLATION of any of the above sections is a fine of not less than $5 nor more than $50, or imprisonment for not more than 30 days. (G.S. 95-24)

MINIMUM WAGE LAW

MINIMUM WAGE RATE. Every employer must pay each of his employees wages at a rate not less than $2.50 per hour, effective January 1, 1978. (G.S. 95-87)

EXCEPTIONS. The N.C. minimum wage does not apply to:
* Establishments covered by the Fair Labor Standards Act (Federal Wage and Hour Law). Workers covered by this law are entitled to a minimum wage of $2.65 an hour, effective Jan. 1, 1978. For further information about the federal law, contact the U.S. Department of Labor, Wage & Hour Division Area Offices, in Raleigh (919) 755-4190, Greensboro (919) 378-5494 and Charlotte (704) 372-0711, Ext. 431.
* Establishments with fewer than four employees.
* Part-time employees working less than 16 hours per week in establishments having three or fewer full-time employees. (G.S. 95-87)
* Federal, state and local government employees, employees under age 16, farm laborers or employees, seafood or fishing industry employees paid on a part-time or piece-rate basis, employees in domestic service, or in private homes or in charitable institutions primarily supported by public funds, volunteer workers in educational, charitable, religious or non-profit organizations, any person under 18 employed by his or her father or mother, inmates of penal, corrective or mental institutions, traveling salespersons, outside salespersons on commission, taxicab drivers and operators, boys' and girls' summer camp employees, newsboys, shoe shine boys, caddies on golf courses, baby sitters (G.S. 95-86) and some seasonal religious assembly or recreational employees who may be paid $2.00 per hour until July 1, 1979. (G.S. 95-88)

PENALTY FOR VIOLATION of any section of the Minimum Wage Law is a fine of not less than $10 nor more than $50, or imprisonment for not more than 30 days. After notification of violation by the Commissioner of Labor, each pay period in which such violation continues constitutes a separate offense. (G.S. 95-94)

UNIFORM WAGE PAYMENT LAW

METHOD OF WAGE PAYMENT. Employees must be paid all wages and tips due them at designated weekly, bi-weekly, semi-monthly or monthly pay periods. The Commissioner of Labor has the authority to assist employees, through inspections, hearings and court action, where necessary, in obtaining payment of wages found due. The employer must notify employees in writing, at the time of hiring, of the rate of pay, policies on vacation and sick leave, and the day, hour and place for payment of wages; make available to employees in writing or through a posted notice maintained in a place accessible to employees, employment practices and policies with regard to vacation pay, sick leave and comparable matters; notify employees in writing, or through a posted notice maintained in a place accessible to employees of any changes in the arrangements specified above prior to the time of such changes; furnish each employee with an itemized statement of deductions made from the employee's wages each pay period. (G.S. 95-161 through 95-172)

VACATION PAY. When it is a matter of employment practice or policy or both, vacation pay shall be considered wages due. (G.S. 95-163(c))

EMPLOYMENT TERMINATION. Upon termination of employment, for any reason, the employer shall pay the employee's earned wages in full not later than the next regular pay date. (G.S. 95-164(b))

EXCEPTIONS. The Uniform Wage Payment Law applies only to employers and employees who are covered by the N.C. Minimum Wage Law. (G.S. 95-162)

PENALTY FOR VIOLATION of the Uniform Wage Payment Law is a fine of not less than $100 nor more than $500 for each separate offense, or imprisonment for not more than 30 days, or both. (G.S. 95-170)

For Further Information:
State Employment Standards Division
North Carolina Department of Labor
4 West Edenton Street, Raleigh, NC 27601
Phone: (919) 733-2152
1/78

John C. Brooks

Commissioner of Labor

State of Ohio
MINIMUM WAGE

DEPARTMENT OF INDUSTRIAL RELATIONS
DIVISION OF WOMEN, MINORS AND MINIMUM WAGE
COLUMBUS, OHIO

JAMES A. RHODES
Governor

HELEN W. EVANS
Director

EFFECTIVE JANUARY 1, 1975

A Minimum Wage of

AUGUST 20, 1976 - $1.90 per hour

JANUARY 1st, 1977 - $2.00 per hour

JULY 1st, 1977 - $2.10 per hour

JANUARY 1st, 1978 - $2.30 per hour

COVERAGE

1. Includes an employer whose annual gross volume of sales made for business done is more than ninety-five thousand dollars and is not covered by the Federal Fair Labor Standards Act.

2. Employers with less than ninety-five thousand dollars gross annual sales in industries covered on December 31, 1973, by Ohio Minimum Wage Orders shall continue to pay the minimum wage as prescribed by IRD 101 or IRD 107.

WAGES

Wages include commissions of which the employer keeps a record and can also include the reasonable cost to the employer of furnishing to an employee board, lodging, or other facilities.

TIPPED EMPLOYEES

For any employee engaged in an occupation in which he customarily and regularly receives more than twenty dollars per month in tips from patrons or others, the employer may pay as a minimum fifty per cent of the minimum wage, if he can establish by his records that for each week where credit is taken, when adding tips received to wages paid, not less than the minimum rate was received by the employee.

LEARNERS RATE
Vocational Students - 180 Days at 80% of Minimum Wage
An employer may pay a learner a wage rate equal to eighty per cent of the minimum wage for a period not to exceed ninety days from the date of employment.

An employee may be employed for only one learner period.

An employer may not have more than two persons or twenty per cent of the persons regularly employed in the establishment in learner status.

HANDICAPPED RATE

To prevent the curtailment of opportunities for employment and avoid undue hardship to individuals whose earning capacity is affected or impaired by physical or mental deficiencies or injuries a sub-minimum wage may be paid, as provided in the rules and regulations set forth by the Director.

OVERTIME

1. An employer shall pay an employee for overtime at a wage rate of one and one-half times the employees wage rate for hours in excess of forty hours in one work week.

2. Restaurant employees are covered under this overtime provision after forty-four hours.

INDIVIDUALS EXEMPT

1. Any individual employed by The United States.

2. Any individual engaged in the delivery of newspapers to the consumer.

3. Any individual employed as an outside salesman compensated by commissions, or individuals employed in a bonafide Executive, Administrative, or Professional capacity.

4. Any individual who works or provides personal services of a charitable nature in a Hospital or Health Institution.

5. Any individual in the employ of a Camp or Recreational area for Children under eighteen years of age and owned and operated by a non-profit organization.

PERMANENT RECORDS TO BE KEPT BY THE EMPLOYER

1. Each employer shall keep permanent records for at least three years, available for transcription and inspection by a duly authorized Deputy of the Department, showing the following facts concerning each employee:
   A. Name
   B. Address
   C. Occupation
   D. Rate of Pay
   E. Amount paid each pay period
   F. Hours worked each day and each work week.

2. Determination of compliance. The records may be opened for inspection or copying at any reasonable time and no employer shall hinder or delay duly authorized Deputy of the Department in the performance of their duties.

FOR FURTHER INFORMATION

Division of Women, Minors and Minimum Wage
2323 West Fifth Avenue
P.O. Box 825
Columbus, Ohio 43216
Phone: (614) 466-4340

THIS POSTER CONTAINS ONLY A SUMMARY
THIS MUST BE POSTED IN A CONSPICUOUS PLACE BY THE EMPLOYER

ABOUT THE AUTHOR

An Atlanta-based labor lawyer, and a partner in the firm of Stokes, Lazarus & Stokes, Arch Stokes received his Doctor of Law Degree from Emory University where he was Managing Editor of the *Law Journal* and Chairman of the Southern Law Review Conference.

As a trial lawyer, judge, and labor lawyer in the Marine Corps, Mr. Stokes tried many cases and negotiated numerous contracts.

A national authority on Labor & Employee Relations Laws as they affect the hospitality, foodservice and convention industries, Mr. Stokes has engaged in televised debates with union leaders, conducted Labor Law seminars all over the United States, and testified before legislative committees. Having worked since his youth at various jobs in the hospitality, foodservice and health care industries, he is familiar with the practical, as well as the legal problems of these industries.

Arch Stokes is an active trial and labor lawyer, representing management in labor litigation, contract negotiations, union campaigns, discrimination suits, and Wage & Hour Law cases. He serves as labor counsel for several hospitality and foodservice companies and public assembly facilities.

Mr. Stokes is a member of both the Labor Relations Law and the Litigation Sections of the American Bar Association, and is listed in *WHO'S WHO IN AMERICAN LAW* and *WHO'S WHO IN THE SOUTH AND SOUTHWEST*. He is also in the Union Internationale des Avocats and active in Confrérie de la Chaine des Rôtisseurs.

182